P9-AOW-183

THE NEW ENGLAND CONSCIENCE

OTHER BOOKS BY AUSTIN WARREN:

Pope as Critic and Humanist (1929)
The Elder Henry James (1934)
Hawthorne ('American Writers Series' 1934)
Crashaw: A Study in Baroque Sensibility (1939)
Rage for Order: Essays in Criticism (1948)
Theory of Literature [in collaboration with René Wellek] (1949)
New England Saints (1956)

The New England Conscience

AUSTIN WARREN

Ann Arbor: The University of Michigan Press

Library of Congress Catalog Card No. 66-11084
Published in the United States of America by
The University of Michigan Press and simultaneously
in Toronto, Canada, by Ambassador Books Limited
Manufactured in the United States of America

For Toni

PREFACE

In 1959 Brandeis University invited me to give a lecture on "The New England Conscience." This lecture I repeated at Vanderbilt and at Syracuse universities and then published in the *Minnesota Review*. Since then, the first and second parts of the lecture have undergone both separation and development. For the rest, the book has been composed as a book, as closely concatenated as I could make it.

After a fashion, it is a companion book to my *New England Saints* of 1956; and the absence of Emerson and the presence of Thoreau in this monograph involve not change of view but equity.

The general scheme has been to show what happened to the New England conscience in the three centuries between 1620 and, say, 1920. For the earlier writers, down to the nineteenth century, I could draw, and have drawn, on the journals of the men studied—journals of self-analysis and resolutions for the self the importance of which William Haller has rightly stressed in the third chapter of his *Rise of Puritanism* (1938). The training by these spiritual account books, as they may be called, is still not extinct among New Englanders; and, in the nineteenth century, they but assume a different form in the journals of Emerson, Alcott, Thoreau, and the Adamses.

With the nineteenth century, the method of my study

changes, however, from analysis of the New Englander's journals to novelists' report and representation of the New England conscience, a conscience still largely formed on journals and other such modes of self-analysis.

I had, as I began the book, not only a method but a hypothesis. Briefly stated, it was that the early Puritans had suffered *for* conscience; that the later New Englanders, especially those of the nineteenth century, suffered *from* conscience. I still think that this is in the main true—though I must grant that Wigglesworth and Cotton Mather do not, in their forms of neuroticism, well back up my theory—and that Garrison and other members of the Abolitionist movement do not well support my view of what happened in the nineteenth century.

But other awarenesses have grown upon me, notably that of types. Bradford and Winthrop are administrators, not clergymen or literary men. And Puritanism (as persons as different as J. A. Froude and Mrs. Stowe both saw) did not affect all psychological types in the same way. It gave strength to many, and they could confidently say, "If God be for us, who can prevail against us?" To others it gave a constant self-searching and quest for evidence of 'election.' They were humbled before the perfection of the Absolute; but the more they were humbled the less they felt any confidence that the Absolute could accept them.

The first part of the book is a general study of conscience; the second, a series of 'case histories.' In writing on authors on whom I have not before written—for example, Henry Adams and E. A. Robinson—the difficulty has been not to write a general, an all-covering, essay; with writers on whom I have repeatedly written—for example, Hawthorne and Henry James—the difficulty has been not to repeat myself. In both cases, I have tried to check myself by remembering that, in the phrase of my old teacher, Irving Babbitt, I am not attempting a "rounded estimate": I am endeavoring to pursue a *motif*, an 'idea.'

I have modernized the spelling and punctuation of my quoted texts; I have also—the reader should be warned—italicized not according to my authors' usage but according to my own emphases, as I would do if I were reading aloud. About this liberty I feel qualms, yet qualms enough allayed by public confession to save me from amending my practice.

In writing this study I have been much and variously helped by the members of a seminar in New England thought which I gave for three years at The University of Michigan; by the support of Professor Warner Rice, Miltonist and friend; by subsidies for 'research' and clerical assistance from the Horace H. Rackham Graduate School; by the labors, intelligence, and sympathy of Mr. Ken Akiyama, Mrs. Rita Blake, Mr. and Mrs. John Murphy, Mr. Jeffrey Mitchell, and most especially Mr. John Conron; by the noble example of my old friend, Wallace Fowlie; by the personal guidance of Robert A. Moore, M.D., and Dom Benedict Reid, O.S.B. My wife has neither typed the manuscript nor read the book, but she has listened to its author's soliloquies anent New England and conscience, and she has sustained him throughout his work by her faith and love.

Ann Arbor, 4 July 1965

CONTENTS

I
CONSCIENCE AND ITS PATHOLOGY

I

The phrase 'New England conscience' I cannot find in any writer before Henry James, who used it in his *Notebooks*—an entry of 1895; yet, as James five years later put the phrase in single quotes, it was presumably an already current phrase. But it does not appear in Hawthorne or in Mrs. Stowe's New England novels; they describe the phenomenon, but never name it. It seems probable that, like 'Puritan,' it was first devised by an outside observer or critic and that it may have first been used pejoratively by those who did not regard the private conscience (if I may be tautological) as both infallible and inexorable.

Such stringency of conscience is, of course, not limited to New Englanders. Matthew Arnold has wise things to say about it in his *Culture and Anarchy* (1869), when he speaks of a "strict conscience" as the pride of English Puritanism—a term which he chronologically extends to include the Nonconformists of his own time. Recommending that the Hebraic conscience be supplemented by the Hellenic consciousness, he appositely quotes the eighteenth-century Anglican Bishop Wilson's maxim, "Never go against the best light you have, [but] take care that your light be not darkness." I understand this maxim to mean—as I think Arnold took it to mean—that conscience is a man's ethical light and moral imperative, and must be followed, but that a second and equal—or better say, almost equal—duty is to regard the conscience as educatable.

Overconscientiousness is not, of course, a purely Protestant phenomenon. The Catholic Church knows it and calls it 'scrupulosity'—a perpetual self-scrutiny, such a concern about details of conduct and purity of intention as leaves the penitent always uncertain whether he has confessed all his sins and whether his absolution is valid, since he is not sure whether he has been truly or adequately enough penitent.

It would be difficult to find a better account of a rigorist 'movement' (as distinct from rigorous individual Christians) than that given in the chapters of Msgr. Ronald Knox's *Enthusiasm*, devoted to the "genius" of seventeenth-century French Catholic Jansenism. Most of the penetrating psychological and theological analyses and judgments of Msgr. Knox (a convert from Low Anglicanism, but a wise and humane judge of the Jesuits' old enemies) apply, with but the slightest alteration, to the New England conscience, which is the British Puritan conscience. This exposition, for example: "If you believe in the Fall as a shattering blow that unmade man to his very essence, then in the first place you are surprised that man should be in position to attain salvation at all—it must be mere grace.... And in the second place you begin to suspect common human virtues; you trace ulterior motives in them, and write them down as 'natural,' useless in God's sight." The "chances are against your being one of the elect, unless your life is heroically given to God as few people's lives are...." It follows that "you must scrutinize your motives carefully to be sure that even your generous actions are dictated by the love of God, not by 'commodity,' friendship, or human respect; that in cases of doubt you must never give yourself the benefit of the doubt but choose the course which is certainly inculpable...."

The protest which Jansenist Port Royal bore against worldliness "was not an asceticism merely; it was a Puritanism; Puritanism is the abstinence from acute pleasure and from careless behavior on the ground that such things are sinful, or so closely bound up with sin that you must avoid them for fear of giving scandal to your neighbors." [1] The moral theology of Port Royal holds that "every action whose conscious motive is something other than love of God and desire for his glory is an action not inspired by grace, and therefore worthless or worse. If I give a birthday present to a child out of love for the child and not explicitly out of love for God, then my motive is not charity (in the theological sense), and it must therefore be put down to some form of *cupidity*."

Nonetheless, the fussy and overexacting conscience is, to my observation and in my judgment, commoner among Protestants than among Catholics, and commonest among those who are "ethnically" rather than theologically Protestant. The seventeenth-century Puritan, like the Orthodox Jew, had an intricate and manifold series of duties prescribed by the infallible Bible and the almost infallible clergy, but the latter-day Protestant has no church to prescribe his major duties and no confessional save his own journals.

II

The 'New England conscience,' it has seemed to me, has had a historical evolution. From the beginning Puritanism (whether Catholic or Protestant) has had its moral rigorism, which, among other purposes, is an army discipline intended to keep a 'dedicated' group—sojourning in alien territory and in lands consecrate to 'false gods'—in that purity of discipline and doctrine, and even, perhaps, diet, necessary to make it tightly cohesive. This is the army discipline of a minority group, a group of volunteers. They have suffered for their convictions; they are prepared to suffer more—to resist actively, or passively, the worst 'other people' (kings, bishops, popular opinion) can do to them. Such men suffer *for conscience*' sake.

Their lot—sometimes unchosen and sometimes rather perversely chosen, by Christians living among pagans, Catholics among Protestants, Puritans among Anglicans, Quakers among Puritans—consisted in being beaten, flogged, imprisoned, exiled, put to death, but it had its reward among those of their own faith and, nowadays, among 'liberals.' In heaven they have obtained the martyr's crown; on earth their names are inscribed in the martyrologies. Their consciences are blameless; they are the objects of persecutions administered by rival theologies and rival ecclesiasticisms.

The 'New England conscience' is not the mark of

those who so suffer, but of those who suffer interiorly *from their own consciences.* They are tormented by doubts and scruples; feel the mixed—and hence impure—motives which prompt them to perform 'good works.' However many 'duties' they have performed, they feel they have never adequately done their Duty. However penitent for their Sin, and their sins, they never feel their contrition adequate.

The immigrant Fathers of New England belonged to the first group. Converted either from religious indifference or from the 'imperfectly reformed' Church of England, they felt no serious doubt of their being, in the language of St. Paul's Epistle to the Romans, 'saints' and the 'elect.' They had suffered imprisonment—or, at any event, silencing—at the mandates of Archbishop Laud, suffered again the journey, which they forever compared to the Israelites' journey through the wilderness to Canaan, which brought them to a place where they could found a truly theocratic state; and at last they were, as they delighted to repeat, a "city set upon a hill," an exemplar to the rest of the world.

The journals of Michael Wigglesworth, an early Harvard graduate, and of Cotton Mather, grandson of immigrant clergy, show much self-chastisement—and, in the case of Mather—many instances of 'special providence'—self-glorifications viewed as signs and angelic, if not divine, visitations; but in both cases—and especially Mather's—it is difficult to distinguish between rhetoric and the desire to edify posterity on the one hand and, on the other, sincere pangs of conscience.

In the next century Jonathan Edwards is the beginning of a new theological and ethical era. No one can read his "Resolutions" and his "Diary" without feeling that they are straightforward wrestlings of the soul; and

I cannot doubt that he was a saint in that more special and Catholic sense unintended by the Pauline and Puritan use of 'saints' as meaning all members of the visible churches of Christ. With Edwards and his *Treatise on the Religious Affections* and with his disciples, Hopkins, Bellamy, and Emmons, the New England conscience as directed against oneself instead of others begins to take shape. It is manifest in Mrs. Marvyn, who sits weekly under the once famous Dr. Hopkins' Edwardsean sermons, is scrupulous in the performance of every duty, yet can never feel that God has elected her to salvation. It is manifest in Dr. Hopkins' own celebrated test of sanctity: that one should be willing to be damned for the glory of God. That was a test which certainly never occurred to seventeenth-century Puritans. Indeed, in the whole period of Edwardsean theology, so distinct from the earlier so-called Calvinism of the immigrant Fathers, one sees conscience turning from the testimony that one is elect to the doubt whether one is not only damned but worthy of damnation.

Unitarians of the benign Boston variety might be expected to mitigate the New England conscience. But here comes another turn of the screw. Legalism and theological system give their own security. To dissolve and discharge these leaves men free to worldliness or to antinomianism or to moralism, but also to self-doubt and self-scrutiny and self-laceration.

Thanks in large measure to his admirably disciplined ancestors, Emerson was an innocent antinomian. Says the father of the Jameses, Emerson "never felt a movement of the life of conscience from the day of his birth till that of his death." [2] And James adds, "If we are still to go on cherishing any such luxury as a private conscience toward God, I greatly prefer for my own part that it should be an evil conscience. Conscience was always intended as a rebuke and never as an exhilaration to the private citizen." Emerson knew youthful depression and a sense of inferiority, but he never knew either of the two religious realizations of man—the sense of sin of the Western Church or the sense of finiteness of the Eastern Church. He was, as William James said in *The Varieties*, once-born.

But Emerson is not a representative of the New England conscience. Eventually, the New England conscience is left faced not with serene and blithe innocence but with the impersonal concept of Duty—not with some naturalistic or humanistic version of Grace but with the Moral Law, a concept and a tyrant more rigid and all-searching, with a rectitude to which one can never attain because it is a perfection both of taste, manners, conduct, and motives. And, as with the ancient Jews, Law does not separate itself from Laws. There are so many high principles to be followed that the high principles themselves conflict, and every case becomes a 'case of conscience'—that is, an attempt to discover which high principle must take precedence over what other high principle. The hedonist may be happy; the saint may say with St. Augustine, "Love and do what you will"; but either the lower or the higher spontaneity is ruled out by the supremacy of Duty.

The Abolitionist Movement was perhaps the last historical moment in which the vigor of the immigrant Fathers showed itself; and the career of Garrison is an instance of a mind at ease in the midst of persecution—at the hand of conservative New Englanders as well as that of foes from without.

Then, deprived of other objective causes for dangerous crusading, the New Englander turns to Education, founds a sequence of Congregationalist colleges from Massachusetts to Ohio, to Iowa, to California; becomes, in the second half of the nineteenth century, the schoolmaster of the enterprising 'barbarians' who settle the Midwest and the Far West.

In the twentieth century, Boston, 'the metropolis' of New England, looks backward, *preserving* the historic churches, houses, and patriotic monuments of an earlier time; or it looks inward and outward, seeking a faith to replace the faith of the Fathers. It cherishes, in the despondency of Robinson, Henry Adams, George Apley, and Oliver Alden, the sense that there was once a Belief which gave meaning to Duty.

III

I wish now to place the 'New England conscience' not historically or locally but philosophically and psychologically; and I shall consider first, the origin and authority of conscience; second, types of conscience; third, the sick conscience and its symptoms: rigor, scrupulosity, indecision, failure of vitality.

"Conscience is God's vice-regent," says the Cambridge Platonist Benjamin Whichcote.[3] God speaks to us through the external Law of His Commandments and Scriptures, an orthodox Jew or Christian would say. He speaks to us also, a Jewish or Christian Humanist would say, through that deposit, accumulation, collection of traditions and tastes and decorous manners which we call civilization. To Bishop Jeremy Taylor, in his *Ductor Dubitantium,* his massive book on casuistical ethics, it seems a matter of relative indifference whether he quotes from the Stoics, or the Platonists, or the eclectic philosopher 'Tully,' or from the Old and New Testament;

and the authority of the Bible is also not very clearly distinguished from the authority of the Greek and Latin Fathers of the Church, whether early or medieval. God speaks also through the Inner Light, which the Quakers contrast with, and to which they give authority higher than, the outer light, even of the Scriptures. The error of Quakerism is, I think, too crude a dichotomy between outer and inner.

The 'vice-regent of God' in the soul is that moral judgment, negative and positive, which, from whatever source, I have actually 'introjected,' made a part of me. To appropriate it, to make it my own, is to make it inner. Conscience is, at best, active apprehension of God as Moral Law or Ethical Person.

The general story of conscience in the 'higher'—and, indeed, 'lower'—religions seems to be approximately the same. 'Conscience'—as consciousness applying itself to ethical judgments, first as judge (and executioner) and then as explorer and guide, going beyond the collective and often unreflective standard of a people—is a late development. The doctrine that conscience (as a form of agency) is innate and intuitive is reconcilable with the evolutionary hypothesis, so ready with copious evidence from history and anthropology. Even among primitive peoples, conscience, as we understand it, is present in germ, in potentiality—just as (whether it ends so or not) it may certainly be conceded that morality begins as *mores*—customs, ways of living and thinking.

Among the Egyptians and Babylonians and even among the Jews and among the Christians, conscience never fully separates itself from the ritual and communal regulations, whether taboos (which doubtless historically come first) or positive injunctions; and I may even think that it is unhealthy and unhistorical that it should. If conscience be represented as the ethical voice of the individual (whether the voice of God within the individual or his own reflective and critical moral insight) pitted against the accumulated and collected 'wisdom,' one has set up a false dichotomy. The 'highest' conscience—the most ethically rarefied intelligence—has not come into being without a history: it starts with, stands on, corrects, refines upon the ethical experience of a nation, a culture, a race. And were it possible for the individual so to divorce himself from the past and the communal, it would be gravely questionable whether such ethical insight were not psychotic. The really wise prophet—though speaking as uttering the word of the Lord as it came to him—finds corroboratory testimony in the initially less articulate conscience of other men.

In his utterances, Jesus often seems to be attacking the Law, that is, the detailed taboos and prescriptions of Deuteronomy and Leviticus; yet he can also say "I come not to destroy but to fulfill" and "not one jot or one tittle shall pass away from the Law till all be fulfilled." Though he can appeal from the prescriptions of the law to its spirit or summarize the Ten Commandments in two: "Love God" and "Love thy neighbor," though he can, by precedent, justify his disciples when, hungry, they pluck and eat corn on the Sabbath, he for the most part follows his people's customs: for example, on the Sabbath he goes to the Synagogue "as he was wont" and he sends the lepers he has healed to the priests to be ceremonially cleansed.

St. Paul is often, in impassioned argument, violently Antinomian, denouncing Jewish legalism in the interests of Christian liberty, but in his frequent administrative moods and epistolary passages, he lays down many prescriptions and taboos—for example, his requirement that, in church, women have their heads covered "for fear of the angels."

Conscience is a Platonic 'form'; its 'matter' is the accumulated specificity of moral cases and judgments. Conscience is a lamp, but a lamp filled with oil. The 'wise virgins,' whose lamps are filled with oil, are not dependent for it on sudden and fortuitous supplies miraculously provided by immediate revelation: their regular supply comes from the accumulated spiritual and moral resources of their nation, as collected in the Scriptures and in oral traditions such as reach classic form in the *Pirke Aboth*, the 'sayings of the fathers.'

Moral wisdom would seem to require us to start not from a hypothetical and impossible clean sweep of the board, to begin again as though none has ever lived before us, but rather to start with the views and principles and maxims current in our environment and to proceed from there, rejecting those which our experience or observation prove ill-founded.

IV

Of the varieties of conscience, it seems easiest to say, flatly, with the elder Henry James, that there is no such thing as a 'good' conscience: the function of conscience is always to convict us of sin, so that (James would argue) sinful, unavoidably, as individuals, we may renounce all claims to personal righteousness or merit and betake ourselves to humble and hearty and anonymous identification with mankind. And St. Paul, for all his moments of bragging ("God forbid that I should boast; but, if any man can boast, I . . ."), seems on his side.

Doubtless, self-castigation, repentance, the determination to lead a new life which must be bound up with true penitence, are the chief functions of conscience. Yet I hesitate to deny that there is such a thing as a good conscience—an approximate parallel to good health. Like good health, one does not think of it, still less speak of it: indeed, the chief evidence of its presence is the absence of aches, pains, torments. It seems easiest to think of a good conscience in Catholic terms. There is, familiar to one, a chart of mortal sins and venial sins. One has committed no mortal sin, or having done so he has repented, gone to confession, been absolved. Of his venial sins he takes note, attempts to conquer those which are habitual. But his efforts go toward the establishment of good habits, not toward 'dwelling upon' his sins, not toward introspection, still less, retrospection.

This is a kind of 'good conscience' which does not depend on subjective judgments, but—so to speak—on health certificates issued by spiritual physicians in good and regular standing.

The 'bad conscience' may similarly be construed on Catholic lines or on Protestant. The Catholic conscience is bad when impenitent or unshriven. The Protestant conscience brings a total charge of natural depravity: we are all "miserable sinners, and there is no health in us." [4] There is no *health in us:* there is health only in recognizing that our very natures are malformed, sick, beyond recovery, or partial recovery; in renouncing our natural selves. We must then accept the 'imputed righteousness' of Christ, or we must be 'converted' from facing toward self to facing toward Christ, or we must, after the first stage of conversion, press on in search of the 'second blessing,' 'holiness,' or 'sanctification' (which seems to be the rightist Protestant equivalent of the Catholic freedom from mortal sin, only a permanent equivalent, not one of falling and being reinstated).

The 'bad conscience' may also be equated with the conscience so dulled and blunted, whether by habitual sin or false doctrine, that it ceases to operate—perhaps we should call it the defunct conscience. Unused, unheeded, it has atrophied—no longer functions. This conscience—'bad' or 'defunct'—is the torpid, the inactive conscience. Cease to listen to conscience, and it ceases to speak, or speaks so faintly as to be inaudible.

Lastly, there is the sick conscience. It is morbid, overactive, feverish; it is unable to obtain any objectivity, to make any distinctions between the 'chief commandments' and those lesser ones which are subsumable under them. The more one shifts attention from recognizable virtues and good acts to the 'good will,' 'intention,' 'motive,' the more one is in danger of falling sick of conscience—which, in its healthy state, must somehow keep a balance between the objective (the act, the virtue) and the subjective (the intention, the motive). Always to be taking one's spiritual pulse is neurotic; to refuse ever to take it—or, better, have it taken—is moral stupidity and arrogance.

V

The sick conscience is rigid, inflexible, tries to reduce all morality (and all life is moral) to a single principle; rejects consequences, seen or foreseen as a part of the moral act; admits of no 'mixed motives,' even though benevolence be one; is disposed to confuse virtue with merit.

Kant taught that "the requirement of the moral command must be propounded and fulfilled *solely for its own sake*." He does not appeal to what a man already wishes on other grounds, but "demands an act of the will which has its worth in itself only, and the only true moral action is one in which such a command is fulfilled without regard to any other consequences." "The fundamental characteristic of the *contrast between duty and inclination* lies deeply rooted in his system.... The empirical impulses of human nature are, therefore, in themselves, ethically indifferent; but they become bad as soon as they oppose the demand of the moral law, and the moral life of man consists in realizing the command of duty in the warfare against his inclinations." [5] Indeed, virtue is not virtue unless it represents duty done in opposition to inclination; the practical consequence of which would be that if you found yourself enjoying the doing of something—such as teaching, or studying, or writing, or talking with friends—you must be doing something unvirtuous: I am tempted to add or *sinful;* but 'sinful' is a specifically theological judgment or category which Kant would not, I think, have invoked. Perhaps he did not suppose all of life to fall under moral categories; perhaps he thought that some acts are 'morally indifferent.' Was he not deriving pleasure from reading his travel books, or walking with his poodle? Perhaps these were viewed as such recreation as would better fit him to resume his studies with more intense concentration and consequence.

It appears to me (as to the philosophers critical of 'duty for duty's sake') that the Kantian doctrine fails to distinguish between 'virtue' and 'merit.' When I was a boy in school, my report card had at least two categories; my grade in each course (this was an attempted estimate of my achievement, either relative to that of others in my class or to some postulated norm of what, at my age, boys might be expected to do—their knowledge, accuracy, ability to express themselves orally and on paper), and then also my grade for 'effort,' which theoretically at least, might be in inverse relation to the grade for 'achievement.' To get a passing grade in mathematics might require far more effort than to win the highest distinction in literature and language. How to grade 'effort' with any degree of objectivity seems difficult, and yet better than what, as a teacher, I am now asked to do, or feel called to do—that is, to combine my judgments in a single grade. All I can objectively do is to grade 'achievement,' and, if I have observed improvement in the course of a semester, it is still improvement in achievement. The Kantian system, on the contrary, seems to give but a single grade, and that based on 'effort.'

My illustration is overlong, but I want to register my judgment that virtue is, like music or poetry, something which can be recognized and rewarded, without regard to whether or not it was accompanied by conflicts.

Certainly too, virtue may be so expected, like manners or ability to think, to come to approach the habitual. And its being, or becoming, habitual (something which makes it often seem to others 'spontaneous' or 'second nature') ought not to rule out its claim to being virtuous. It is certainly a crude conception of 'freedom of will' which makes that freedom consist in one's having, at every moment, to choose what kind of man one wants to be. The virtuous self is one with which virtuous habits are habitual, whether that state, that constitution, was arrived at after long struggle, or little and brief. But if that be so, the aim of the good man is to foster his virtuous inclinations and to habituate his unvirtuous inclinations to following the law of virtue till they present less and less resistance to such following. But I cannot say that all my inclinations are hostile to virtue—still less, keep alive the unvirtuous ones in order that I gain the daily merit of fighting them.

And now it is clear that the extreme forms of Protestant doctrine, specifically Calvinism (or Puritanism, as it was commonly called by nineteenth-century American writers), really and seriously do say what I have just said I cannot say. I have spoken in the vein of Aristotle and Christian humanism, whether Catholic, Orthodox, or Anglican, of 'good inclinations' and bad inclinations. But Calvinism takes no such view of man. Without grace, he is totally depraved. Whatever seems to be virtuous in an unregenerate man is appearance or *natural* inclination: not proceeding from a good will, his virtues are, as Tertullian said, "but splendid vices."

President Edwards demonstrated this to his own satisfaction and to the admiration of those who admire (as I do) his self-consistency and dialectical rigor, in *The Nature of True Virtue*. 'Natural affection,' as that of parents for their children, is only natural—we share it with the animals and birds; being generous to those who are generous to us, "Do not even the Gentiles do the same?" But to rise above such reciprocities to loving our enemies, to Edwards' "disinterested benevolence," these are things supernatural, made possible only by the grace of regeneration.

Kantian ethics, stripped of theological language and having no recourse to supernatural aid, restates rigidly and baldly the Calvinistic opposition between true virtue and pleasure. Whether there is a historical and causal relation between it and Puritanism I don't know, probably not. But both state a half-truth. Virtue is not doing what I want to do. Equally, however, it is not necessarily doing what I *don't* want to do. Neither my pleasure nor my lack of pleasure can be the criterion of virtue—

which, whatever else it is, must be objective enough to withstand identification with *effort,* or merit.

Much of the falsity of the Protestant ethics lies in just what—whether in its popular or its philosophic form—it has prided itself on: its concern with self and subjectivity. Concern with *my* motives, *my* intentions, *my* conscience is always in danger of becoming more concerned with me than with God and my neighbor, with that whole vast other world. Egoism—refined subjectivity—is morally more dangerous partly because more subtle, than plain frank egotism or selfishness.

Von Hügel, one of the wisest, bids us to "get rid of all self-occupation. I don't mean self-examination for conscience' sake, though this too can be overdone. But self-oblivion is a splendid thing; move out of yourself, let in God." [6]

One of the most penetrating comments ever made on rigorism in general, Mrs. Stowe makes on the Edwardsean variety: "There is a ladder to heaven whose base God has placed in human affections, tender instincts, symbolic feelings, sacraments of love. . . ." The highest step of the ladder "but few selectest spirits ever on earth attain—this Ultima Thule of virtue had been seized upon by our sage as the all of religion. He knocked out every rung of the ladder but the highest, and then, pointing to its hopeless splendor, said to the world, 'Get up thither and be saved.' " [7]

Mrs. Stowe expresses, in her ladder figure, primarily—and consciously, doubtless—the ladder between Heaven and earth which Jacob saw in his dream at Bethel. But she expresses also the spirit of Diotima's discourse in Plato's *Symposium* and—more generally—the view of Christian Humanism of the sort so sympathetically characterized in the first volume of Abbé

Bremond's *Histoire littéraire du sentiment religieux en France*—the volume on St. Francis of Sales and his chief disciples.

Of rigorism in any religion, we can say, I think, that the attempt to impose it as a universal rule on a whole community (such as the Massachusetts Bay Colony) is bound to fail. Port Royal was, after all, primarily a 'religious order,' a community of nuns and allied clerics. When you try to apply it to a whole society it inevitably breaks down after the Founding Fathers die and after the first fires of ardor, the religious experiences of men who have wrestled with God for their faith, turn into the imposition on future generations (who have not known danger, exile, inner torment, conversion, inner peace labored for and won) of formulae of behavior and attitude drawn up not on the basis of things they have seen and heard but as regularized and ritualized transcripts of those original experiences.

VI

Scrupulosity is a natural consequence, it would seem, of the constant self-analysis of one's motives. If *intention* (or motivation) be viewed as the only thing that morally or religiously matters, and *consequences* (or even the contemplation of *consequences* as a part of one's intention) be viewed as mutually exclusive conceptions of morality, then scrupulosity—the microscopic study of 'should I; shan't I?'—seems almost inevitable—as a kind of laxly or grossly pragmatic view may seem the natural consequence of the *utilitarian* (or *consequential*) view. Scrupulosity in all areas seems a form of invalidic perfectionism—a forever taking of one's pulse, a disposition not to act at all if there is danger of one's acting unwisely. Large general principles get lost sight of in the concern not to make errors in detail. (To which, of course, the scrupulous man will naturally reply that every detail is the exemplification in small of some principle. When he is told by another, "We must of course agree on *fundamentals,* but can agree to disagree on 'matters indifferent,'" he will immediately counter, "There are no matters indifferent.")

But *scrupulosity* is a pathological form of rigorism or of conscientiousness—though, in saying this a son of the Puritans feels it necessary, in honesty, to add that it is, like neuroticism, on the boundary line between disease and a sin which looks like virtue. Hence the difficulty of curing the scrupulous, for you must do so without, to their minds, demolishing the virtue which they consider 'conscientiousness'—just as you must cure their conception that *duty* and *pleasure* are mutually exclusive without destroying a sound and balanced sense of moral obligation. The difficulties are partly semantic, certainly, but not entirely so.

Helpful to this end is F. H. Bradley's celebrated essay, "My Station and Its Duties" (*Ethical Studies,* 1876). Bradley may, in this essay, be partly ironic, and he is not, I judge, stating his final stand; but, whatever his intention, his essay is a brilliantly reasoned attack on all ultrarefined, self-scrutinizing forms of rigoristic ethics, a wholesome statement of an ethics within the realm of possibility. I may have all sorts of hypothetical duties, but duty, however far it may reach, begins with the duties set by my family relations, my profession. "My *heart* I am not to think of, except to tell by my work whether it is in my work, and one with the moral whole." "To be moral, I must *will* my station and its duties. . . . No objective organism, the systematized moral world, is the reality of the moral will; my duties on the *inside* answer to due functions on the outside."

This, I think, is drawing the *sting* out of *duty* by representing it not as something alien to what I am and can do but as the faithful, intelligent willed performance of what my nature, my talents, and my 'station' in society fit me to do. By doing my real, as distinct from imaginary, duty, I have the double pleasure of expressing myself and being of use to society. Bradley's essay leaves me unsatisfied: the transcendental, the romantic, the heroic, the religious aspects of ethics have disappeared. I feel as I used to when I heard Irving Babbitt (to whose intense and crusading spirit it seemed false) commend his New Humanism as asking only that men "be decent and sensible." But it is a good temporary therapeutic.

One of the most painful—probably, but one of the most 'human'—vexations of 'scrupulosity' is to find that, even when doing good and generous things, my virtues are never unmixed, never pure. What a blessed relief, I think, would it be to feel one unmixedly disinterested and pure motive. Yet I can see the sin which underlies it: wanting to be God, I am impatient with myself—an impatience which (as the great Fénelon points out) is at least as bad as being impatient with others. I incline to think it is worse, since we can be tolerant of others from some quasi- or pseudo-Divine tolerance with human stupidity and frailty; while to be impatient with ourselves is all too likely to be a Luciferian pride, a finite rage at our not being the Infinite God.

VII

Scrupulosity almost invariably leads to indecision. The sick conscience is irresolute: it says 'shall I?,' 'shan't I?,' 'ought I?,' 'ought I not?' till all energy is exhausted and nothing decided. But either one does or one doesn't. If time and energy be exhausted in determining, one has still acted by not acting, or by frenzied atomistic acts which not only counteract each other but prevent any steady, constant attention and action. On this topic, materialist and idealist agree.

Says Hobbes: "After men have been in deliberation till the time of action approach, if it be not then manifest what is best to be done, 'tis a sign the difference of motives, the one way and the other, are not great. Therefore, not to resolve them is to lose the occasion by weighing of trifles, which is pusillanimity." And James Martineau: "Conscientiousness is no security of energy, and is even apt to degenerate into a certain weakness of character." [8] Emerson wrote of his own time: "Every age, like every human body, has its own distemper.... Our [New England] forefathers walked in the world and went to their graves tormented with the fear of sin and the terror of the Day of Judgment. These terrors have lost their force; and our torment is Unbelief, *the Uncertainty as to what we ought to do; the distrust of the value of what we do....*" [9]

In his *Spiritual Letters*, Fénelon gives the best advice I know to overscrupulous and hence irresolute consciences: "As to your actions, if they are good in themselves, reject all questionings as to the motives whence they spring; otherwise you will never have done: you will get worried, be disheartened, and, while cavilling uselessly over motives, you will forget to act." "Occupy yourself with your daily duties: controlling expenses, watching over the welfare of your household, fulfilling the just claims of society so as to edify all around you without ever talking to them about religion." "Keep to your real duties; be quiet and recollected, diligent in your business. . . ." [10]

I need add merely that 'spiritual letters,' a genre at which the French—and especially Fénelon—excel, are not intended to be catholic or general epistles: they are addressed to a specific person and his situation; they are, in the best sense of the word, 'casuistical.' What he gives in these sentences is not advice to the callous or careless; it is the best advice I know to irresolute, overscrupulous, sick consciences.

A Jesuit, Father Ramière, defending the book of another Jesuit, Father Caussade, a great spiritual master albeit tainted with Quietism, or susceptible of being read Quietistically, says: After "having done all that depends on our own efforts we will abandon ourselves completely to God for the rest." [11] But the 'scrupulous' mind asks, How do we ever know whether we have done all we can; have made all the effort we can? This is the rocky question upon which the scrupulous wreck themselves. Yet if we don't ask that question we may (it seems to me) fall into a self-indulgent and easily satisfied morality or a pseudo-mystical antinomianism.

These questions must be asked, but the answering ought not to be too protracted or subjectively agonizing. As I write of Scylla and Charybdis, I am unavoidably reminded of Aristotle's *Nichomachean Ethics*, a book which leaves me always with mixed feelings. It treats life as a practical art, in which common sense and intuitive judgment, rather than rigorous reduction of everything to a single principle, must be our guides. Until we reach the final book, a kind of appended apostrophe to the Contemplative Life, we are given no other axiom than that of virtue as a mean between two extremes: we must be neither too miserly nor too prodigal, neither too foolhardy nor too cautious. But, by temperament, most men incline to one extreme or the other. And when, through self-examination or the advice of wise friends, we discover our temperamental imbalance, we must, by way of corrective, school ourselves to counteracting temperament by leaning to its opposite.

This is all sensible; and Aristotle's *Ethics* is the most sensible book on the subject I know. But how do I judge the degree of my imbalance, and how judge the degree of leaning in the direction opposite to inclination? Not to mention my doubt whether the perfectly well-balanced nature is what we should set as our goal.

These are questions which Aristotle, who does not view ethics as an 'exact science,' leaves unanswered—which he can the more readily do since he doesn't have to think of the kind of balance needed by the artist in comparison with the kind of balance needed by any other kind of man than the *honnête homme*, the gentleman.

The answer is certainly that virtue is an art and not a science. It cannot be reduced to rigoristic simplicity nor arrived at by self-analyzing the self.

In matters of conscience, it seems to me that we should never rely solely on our own judgment. We all need the help of what the French call 'spiritual directors'—who, in our time, may be priests or psychiatrists (happy is the man who can have the help of both), or just 'wise' and 'mature' men and women. There are not enough proper 'spiritual directors' to go around; and 'wise' books do not really take their place, since all spiritual direction must be, in the good sense, casuistical. But we must secure the best guidance we can—that of persons not bound up with us personally, persons of general intelligence and good will—at once attached (since we are under their direction) and detached (since our relation is not, in the ordinary sense, personal).

A 'spiritual director' is not necessarily a priest—indeed, probably oftener not. His function is to give the clarity of attached detachment to the problems which we see too myopically. He is not to make our decisions for us—that we alone can do, but probably he can aid us to see that decide we must: that indecision and irresolution are weakened and weakening forms of decision and resolution.

In the absence of spiritual direction, some 'guides for the perplexed' may safely be offered the perplexed.

Irresolution of conscience, on the part of a man of good will, seems to arise largely from his temperamental—or temporary—inability to distinguish between major and minor duties: to him, they all seem equally important. Baron von Hügel has given wise counsel: "When I get up feeling I have a hundred things to do—then I know it's all wrong. . . . I leave everything till I am better." If we will wait quietly till the sense of multiplicity subsides, we shall see that the hundred duties are not on the same level of importance. Two or three axioms help here: (1) Some duties must be done today, while others can await their day. (2) Some duties belong to my 'station'—my profession and family life, and those are the duties which 'lie nearest,' not in the sense that I feel them most urgently but that they are minimal, while other duties (including some I may *feel* most) are 'works of supererogation'—meritorious but 'over and beyond the call of duty.' (3) Minor duties should be subsumed under major duties—*species* under *genera*, particulars under generals. This principle does not do away with the need for intelligent casuistry, for we may experience a "collision of duties"—even of major duties, which is to say major loyalties, like that to my family and that to my profession. Still less does it take care of collision between my loyalty to country and my loyalty to God or to mankind, my *conscientia generis humani* (the phrase is that of Tacitus)—such a collision as that experienced by Sir Thomas More or implied (and falsely resolved, one would think) in the American phrase, "My country, right or wrong."

In these ultimate decisions, one is (like the heroes and heroines of Henry James's best novels) 'forced against the wall,' as freedom-loving Isabel Archer is when at the end of *The Portrait of a Lady* she returns to Osmond, or beauty-loving Fleda Vetch is when she refuses minimal concessions of her rigid morality in order to win "Poynton." On this matter of conscience, the heroic counsel must certainly be to rehearse as best one can which one would morally have to choose if one has to choose between two loyalties ordinarily compatible with one another but which at times of crisis, such as are only dimly to be envisaged, may not be.

VIII

As I have been describing—and prescribing for—the sick conscience, I have been describing what is called the 'New England conscience' in its pathology. The Puritan conscience as such is one which gives predominance—an undue predominance—to self-examination and self-discipline. Already in the seventeenth century, we read of New England thrift and industry, of the evil of wasting 'precious time.' Satan finds work for idle hands to do. And into the earlier nineteenth century, the great New England gift of 'faculty' enables the really efficient 'homemaker' to have all her housework done by noon. And of the male, the Harvard historian S. E. Morison, wittily writes, "Your typical Yankee still uses his leisure to think up some labor- or time-saving device, so that he will have more time to think up some other labor and time-saving devices." [12]

The 'New England conscience' appears as a phrase only late in the nineteenth century, and the neuralgic state it describes is also, I think, late. If the Puritan conscience is subject to criticism such as Arnold's, it had its use, its function, perhaps even (in New England, an infertile soil) its necessity. But it survives its function. Thrift, cleanliness, order, become ends in themselves.

The things missing are pleasure, graciousness, joy, love. Neighbors and relatives do kind acts, give good gifts, but do and give so ungraciously that one wishes they wouldn't make the effort. The Lord loveth a cheerful giver. And how the heart of the recipient sinks when, trying to thank the donor, he is told, "I've done no more than my duty"—which turns one into an abstraction to whom an abstraction has been done for abstract motives.

"Love is the fulfilling of the Law." How hard for a Yankee mind to take in. The Law is a duty; and now, instead of real love's taking its place, love is an additional duty.

II
CASE HISTORIES FROM NEW ENGLAND

THE FIRST GOVERNORS
Bradford (1590–1657) and Winthrop (1588–1649)

It seems proper to begin these 'case histories' of New Englanders with two men, both born in Old England and both sincerely religious, who were at the same time executives, called upon by their office to apply Puritanic principles to all manner and degree of practical problems.

They were both conscious of their high responsibilities, not only to the colonies they were founding, but to the Protestant world at large. They were to be, in the Christian metaphor dear to them, 'cities set upon a hill.' As such, it befitted them to walk, and to write. William Bradford left behind him a noble history *Of Plymouth Plantation, 1620–1647*, which, through a series of accidents, remained unpublished till 1856. John Winthrop undoubtedly intended to use his *Journal*, which covers the history of the Bay Colony from 1630 till 1649, as the basis for another such formal narrative as Bradford's.

Both were men of remarkable balance. It is not necessary to agree with their doctrines to perceive this, and to ratify the judgment with which those eligible to vote chose the right leaders. It demonstrates the traditional English common sense that, during their days of hazard, the colonists chose men who, though 'sound' in doctrine, were also practical men, who had memories of the past, a judicious optimism for the future, and the capacity to deal with present emergencies, as they chose, with quick intuitive judgment.

The administrator of an enterprise, whatever its scale, has to have a confidence that he can bring his mind to bear upon a never-ending series of 'cases'—local, interlocal, economic, military—which come before him and have to be decided without undue delay. In a real sense, if the administrator is a man of religious and moral convictions, not a 'politician,' the problem becomes all the more difficult, for he must, as he knows, render an honorable account both to the community which has chosen him and to God.

The healthy conscience, from which it is impossible to separate consciousness, has, like the healthy body, to be strong but lithe; able to be inactive without twitching, to be active without superfluous exertion of energy.

This is probably impossible without discipline; and good as self-discipline may be, it is doubtless better to be exercised by life rather than by rules which, as one has made them for oneself, one can, if he choose, relinquish.

Bradford and Winthrop both knew well, of course,

Foxe's *Book of Martyrs*—which was indeed not even a Puritan monopoly, for it was read during meals at Little Gidding, the closest approach to an Anglican monastery which existed in the seventeenth century; but there is nothing of the neurotic 'martyr' about them: they are not passive, and their personal troubles are either mentioned in passing or are the occasion for rousing themselves to action.

I

Bradford, of Yorkshire stock, was the son of a yeoman, but, early an orphan, he was put in the charge of his uncles. At twelve, he became a constant reader of the Bible, in the Geneva version, forsook St. Helen's, the parish church of his native village, to walk to hear the Puritan preacher at Babworth, eight miles away, and not much later joined a group of young Puritans who met at the house of William Brewster in Scrooby. In these actions he was angrily opposed by his uncles and scoffed at by his neighbors, but all in vain. In 1606 this group was organized as a separate Congregational church. These Separationists, mostly of the humbler sort, had no designs on the State Church, the National Church, the Established Church of England—while the main body of people called Puritans did: they wanted to make the Church of England Presbyterian, like the Church of Geneva or the Church of Scotland; to carry the Reformation through to its Calvinistic end—to get rid of bishops and the Liturgy, then to take possession of the National Church and force all Englishmen to be Puritans. The Separatists wanted to divorce the union between Church and state and dissolve 'the Church' into a series of individual congregations.

The much smaller and humbler group (which we

now call Pilgrims)[1] was more readily open to attack, and they decided to migrate to Holland, a country known for its religious toleration. They betook themselves first to Amsterdam and then, after a year, to Leyden. There was much for them to contend with, for they were from "plain country villages," most of them farmers, and they had not only to learn a new language but to learn new ways of supporting themselves by "such trades and employments as they best could"—mostly, as Bradford did, by some form of cloth-making, the chief industry of Leyden. Bradford discusses the "Reasons and Causes" why migration from Holland seemed desirable—the most important, perhaps, the danger of corruption to their children and the fear of the children's losing their language and nationality.

Their enterprise was occasioned by every kind of difficulty. The financing of the voyage and the subsequent livelihood of the Pilgrims were undertaken by London 'Adventurers' (or promoters, as we might now call them). The terms were hard—a fifty-fifty division of profits between the 'Adventurers' and the Pilgrims, the latter of whom were to live for seven years in a kind of communism. The Pilgrims were to have no days to work for themselves and were not to own their own houses. This communism broke down before the seven years, and Bradford comments expressly on the ineffectiveness of expecting able men and married to work for the aged and the single.

All the planning seems to have been badly done during the period before Bradford became governor. The immigrants' knowledge of New England was entirely dependent on a small book and a map contained in it—Captain John Smith's *Description of New England* (London, 1616). And in order to have crops to sustain them during the winter, they should have reached New England in June, instead of which (chiefly because of wrangling among the Adventurers) they did not land till November.

Arrived, after a long voyage, at Plymouth, the men of the "Mayflower" went ashore to reconnoiter and came upon some Indian graves and near them, buried in the sand, some baskets filled with Indian corn. On another occasion, they found both corn and beans, which they took, "purposing" to give the Indians "full satisfaction when they should meet with any of them . . ."—which they did; and so they had seed to plant their corn the next year. This Bradford notes as "a special providence of God."

Bradford's twenty-three-year-old wife had accompanied him on the "Mayflower," but, during the last, and nearly week-long, of the men's exploratory trips made in a shallop, his wife fell overboard from the ship, though it was anchored in a quiet harbor. It seems likely that she had killed herself, possibly fearful of the prospect of wilderness ahead. Bradford made an entry in his pocket notebook of her death, painful to him whatever its reason, and bent himself with single-minded energy to his work.

Before they left the "Mayflower," the male colonists drew up a *Compact*, a brief written constitution to which forty-one signers subscribed their names—a covenant "by virtue hereof to enact, constitute and frame such just and equal Laws, Acts, constitutions, and offices . . . as shall be thought most meet and convenient for the general welfare of the community."

The most difficult time for the Pilgrims was the first winter, during which, by reason of scurvy and other diseases occasioned by the long voyage and partly by reason of the poor housing, scant diet, and winter cold, the deaths were numerous. At the end of that first winter, but half of the passengers who reached Cape Cod survived, including but a few of the women. In the time of most distress, there were but six or seven sound persons; these six or seven valiantly looked after the ill, among whom was Bradford.

With the aid of Squanto, a friendly Indian who had sojourned in England, the Pilgrims made a compact with Massasoit, chief of the tribe, an honorable statement of a common standard for both white men and red, in consequence of which there was no war in Bradford's time.

In May, Bradford, as magistrate, performed the first marriage in the place, following the custom of the Low Countries and Scriptures (Ruth 4), "nowhere found in the Gospel to be laid on the ministers as part of their office."

The Plymouth colony had, indeed, ill luck with clergymen. Their liberal and beloved pastor at Leyden, the Reverend John Robinson, was never able to make the journey. They had a variety of misfits, from an Anglican, Lyford, who was sexually immoral and a double-dealer, to Roger Williams, "having," Bradford says, "many precious parts but unsettled in judgment." Happily, they were so near to being a layman's church that these troubles did not disturb them: their lay elders were perfectly competent to preach the Sunday sermons.

The dramatic episode of Morton's "plantation" at Mount Wollaston, or Merrymount, Bradford deals with in sensible enough terms. The drinking of "both wine and strong waters in excess," the dancing with Indian women, the maypole are duly reported in *Of Plymouth Plantation;* but Bradford chiefly reprimands the sale of firearms to the Indians, not a friendly office to other Englishmen.

The Pilgrims, like the Puritans, did not celebrate Christmas or Easter—on the ground that the Scriptures give no date for either.[2] In 1621 arrived in Plymouth an unexpected ship bringing thirty-five unexpected augmentations to the community—most of them "lusty, young men, and many of them wild enough." On Christmas day, Bradford (who commonly speaks of himself in the third person as governor) "called them out to work as was used." But most of them, excusing themselves, said "it went against their consciences to work on that day." So they were excused from work. But at noon they were found in the street at play, openly; some pitching the bar and some at stool-ball [something like cricket]. . . ." The governor took away their equipment and told them "that it was against *his conscience*, that they should play and others work. If they made the keeping of it a matter of devotion, let them keep their houses; but there should be no gaming or reveling in the streets. Since which time, nothing hath been attempted that way, *at least openly*." [3]

Evidence of Bradford's tolerance and courtesy in matters he deemed nonessential is perhaps best illustrated by his entertainment in 1650 of a Jesuit priest, Father Druillettes, missionary to the Abenaki Indians. Bradford, recollecting that the day was Friday, served fish for dinner.

Says Cotton Mather, in the great *Magnalia*, Bradford "was a person for study as well as action." In 1632 Winthrop, who deemed his fellow governor "discreet and grave," remarked his knowledge of Hebrew; but this study was more possible in his last years, when he wrote, "Though I am grown aged, yet I have had a longing desire to see with my own eyes something of that most ancient language and holy tongue in which the Law and oracles of God were writ, and in which God and angels spake to the holy patriarchs of old time...."

II

John Winthrop, of Groton, was the grandson of a London cloth merchant who had money enough to buy, at the Reformation, a part of a confiscated monastery in Suffolk and become a country gentleman. He was schooled by the vicar of a nearby church and at fifteen went to Trinity College, Cambridge, for two years. Somewhere, at Cambridge if not before, he became a Puritan. His brief notes on his religious experience show his arguments with himself about shooting game, about overeating. The conclusion of his alternation of over-indulgence in the pleasures of this world and abstinence is almost a motto for his life. He "who would have sure peace and joy in Christianity must not aim at a condition retired from the world and free of temptations but to know that the life which is most exercised with trials and temptations is the sweetest and will prove the safest. For such trials as fall within compass of our callings, it is better to arm and withstand them than to avoid and shun them."

He married at seventeen, and his first wife, not a Puritan, bore him six children in ten years and died. In less than a year he married again; his second wife died in just a year. In his old age he married for a fourth time and by his fourth wife had a son.

But his *real* wife, as one is tempted to call her—the

wife who was his loved helpmate for thirty years—was Margaret Tyndal, whom he married at thirty.

In his thirties he studied law, became one of Suffolk county's justices of the peace, in 1627 became common attorney for the Court of Wards and Liveries, an archaic institution which required his spending something like four months of a year living as a bachelor in London's Inner Temple.

In 1629 Charles I dissolved Parliament, not to hold it again till 1640, and Archbishop Laud was rising to power in both Church and state. The hope of any Low Church domination of Anglicanism seemed remote. But the Puritans could not, like the Pilgrims and other Separatists, think, consciously at least, of breaking with the Church.

Just before Charles dissolved Parliament, a royal charter was granted to the governor and Company of Massachusetts Bay, and Winthrop, not earlier sanguine about migration, became more and more interested.

Winthrop's legal mind—if one wants to call it that—drew up, with the advice of Puritan clergy, the arguments pro and con migration—arguments economic as well as religious. His chief deterrent was an argument with which the Bay Colony Puritans were later taunted by those of their persuasion who stayed at home. Was emigration not a form of escape? One of his friends frankly told him, "The Church and Commonwealth here at home hath more need of your best ability in these dangerous times than any remote plantation," and he himself, in his table of pros and cons wrote, "It will be a great wrong to our own Church and country to take away the *good* people. . . ."

The Massachusetts Bay Company was a trading corporation, and, like other such corporations with domains overseas, normally met in London. But in this instance no place of meeting was specified, and the Company, Winthrop concurring, decided that it might be within the Colony itself. It is difficult to suppose that the King and his advisers intended or anticipated this. In taking this course, Winthrop is acting like a lawyer, as Newman did in his famous Tract 90, which reads the 39 Articles word by word—for example, the Anglican Church rejects the *Romish* doctrine of Purgatory, not any doctrine of Purgatory, as a truly Catholic one. But there may well be a matter of conscience in substituting a legal or *in totidem verbis* reading for a reading by intention or probability or historical context.

In April 1630, when Winthrop, already chosen first governor, was ready to sail, his wife was pregnant, had as well a two-year-old child; it seemed best to leave her in England for the immediate present. But to this temporary separation are due letters of Winthrop's which, better than anything I know, evince with what sincerity and ease the Puritan mind moved from family love and practical affairs to religion.

"Mondays and Fridays, at five of the clock at night, we shall meet in spirit till we meet in person. Yet if all these hopes should fail, blessed be our God that we are assured we shall meet one day, if not as husband and wife, yet in a better condition."

"Thou must be sure to bring no more company than so many as shall have full provision for a year and a half, for, though the earth here be very fertile, yet there must be time and means to raise it; if we have corn enough, we may live plentifully. Yet all these are but the means which God hath ordained to do us good by: our eyes must be towards Him, Who, as He can withhold blessings from the strongest means, so He can give sufficient virtue to the weakest.... Remember to come well furnished with linen, woolen, some more bedding,—brass, pewter, leather bottles, drinking horns, etc.; let my son provide 12 axes of several sorts . . . and some augers great and small, and many other necessaries which I can't now think of,—wax candles, soap, and store of beef suet, etc. Once again, farewell, my dear wife."

Winthrop brought with him four hundred men, women, and children, and six hundred more were on their way. This, the 'Great Migration,' was an undertaking which, by its very size, was quite different from that of Bradford, who, to the end of his life, would have wished the Plymouth colony to be a somewhat expanded country village.

The transition was a multiplied version of that suffered at Plymouth. Salted meat as a prolonged diet produced scurvy, and, though game birds were plentiful, few knew how to shoot them—or to shoot deer. New England summers were hotter, New England winters colder, than those at home. Between the cold and the meager rations, two hundred died the first winter, and others returned to England.

Here Winthrop's courage, the courage of a leader, shows itself. What weakens some arouses others: I think of F. D. Roosevelt and Sir Winston Churchill. Winthrop, a man in his early forties when he became leader, was invigorated. "I like so well to be here," he wrote his wife, still in England, "as I do not repent my coming; and, if I were to come again, I would not have altered my course, though I had forseen all these afflictions. I never fared better in my life, never slept better, never had more content of mind."

The first winter was the hardest. In the spring Winthrop set his staff of servants to building him a stone house on his large farm near the Mystic River. But his thoughts were chiefly how to make the colony economically well by discovering what they could ship to England in return for what they had to buy from England. The standbys were, naturally, at first fur and fish, but the Colonists were able to add lumber, Indian corn, and cattle.

When, in 1631, Winthrop's wife and family arrived, the 'first fruits' of Yankee abundance came in the form of a communal 'Harvest Home' offering of "hogs, kids, venison, poultry, geese, partridges."

The economic problem temporarily solved, Winthrop had yet one more difficult. The Puritan state has often been called a 'theocracy' and the Puritan clergy its rulers: the Jews were ruled by judges guided by prophets like Samuel before they revolted and demanded a king, as other nations had. In a very real sense, the clergy did rule the state, both because only Church members—whose claims to join the Church, based upon their account of their 'religious experience,' a testimony judged valid or invalid by the clergy—could vote or hold office, and because the General Court, consisting of the governor and his assistants, did not differentiate between "judicial and legislative functions" or between religio-moral and civic commandments. It was this failure which Roger Williams attacked when he said that the state could rightfully punish only violations of the Second Table of the Law (that is, matters like stealing). That the clergy should literally occupy state offices as did Cardinal Richelieu or Archbishop Laud was surely unnecessary when they could influence or control the voters and the voter-elected government.

Having repeated this often-repeated view of the theocracy (most damagingly stated by Brooks Adams, Henry's brother, in *The Emancipation of Massachusetts*, emancipation, as Adams means, from the power of the Congregational clergy), and quite aware of the 'logic' just outlined, I can still see the slight but real gap allowed in practice to a 'first governor,' a man of Winthrop's English—as well as colonial—prestige. The clergy were not always of one mind, and, though he was ordinarily elected governor at the annual election, he had a few rivals—men of different temperament from his.

As long as he lived he was, I do not doubt, the most conciliatory and moderate and mediating of the alternates. Sir Henry Vane was to the left of him; Endicott and Dudley to his right.

Protest though the Puritans might that they had separated from England but not from the English Church, they no sooner reached America than they adopted a system of church government chiefly Congregational, but partly Presbyterian; and by their very migration they had testified to a kind of separatism and perfectionism: the church was not for all men, like Catholicism and Anglicanism, but for the 'saints,' for those who believed themselves to be, and were able to convince the clergy that they were, among the 'elect.'

And protest though the Puritans might, it was difficult to make it clear to religious speculatives and experimentalists that an experimental and religious colony cannot find a place for them all. England during the Commonwealth had its fill of 'splinter-groups'; and New England's chiefest trouble—and Winthrop's—came from these groups—some (like Milton in England and Roger Williams in New England) ultimately churches of one member. Roger Williams, Anne Hutchinson, her brother-in-law, the Reverend John Wheelwright, and the Quakers were all ultimately witnesses to the Inner Light, who, though they paid service to the Bible (which all, including Mrs. Hutchinson, could quote effectively), might be said either to follow their own—not any standard or communal—interpretation of it, or (like Robert Barclay in his *Apology for the Quakers*) frankly put the Bible second to the Inner Light as authority for religious truth.

Anne Hutchinson and Roger Williams have an especial attraction for many in our time, and the Puritans seem harshly intolerant of them and other individualists and cruel in banishing them from the Bay Colony. But we live—and have long lived—in a society obviously conformist and now so 'affluent' that we can waste food, money, time, and even lives: can bomb and bribe 'underprivileged peoples,' and can readily outdo the Puritans in spiritual arrogance. Such 'tolerance' is all but impossible—certainly impracticable—to a newly established community, struggling to maintain itself against enemies from without and from inner dissensions which can disturb even the elementary requirements of a body politic.

But having said this, I must add that Winthrop, by conscience, was a humble man and desirous of the utmost moderation he could manage in his treatment of those from whom he dissented.

In 1636 Winthrop records in his *Journal* that Sir Henry Vane and Hugh Peters found factions among the people, some adhering to himself, some to Dudley, "the former carrying matters with more lenity and the latter with more severity, and that a meeting was called at which the four 'statesmen' and three of the most prominent clergy, including the Rev. John Cotton were present." Winthrop, told of several occasions in which he had "dealt too remissly in point of justice," answered that "his speeches and carriage had been in part mistaken" but that it was indeed his judgment that, "in the infancy of plantation, justice should be administered with more lenity than in a settled state, because people were then more apt to transgress, partly through oppression of business and other straits, but if it might be made clear to him that it was an error, he would be ready to take up a stricter course." The reverend clergy were then desired to consider the question (were appointed, Americans would now say, a *committee* to study the matter and report their judgment). The next day they took the opposite view to Winthrop's, adjudged "that strict discipline, both in criminal offences and in martial affairs, was more needful in plantations than in a settled state, *as tending to the honor and safety of the Gospel.*" Whereupon, with reasonable sincerity I suppose, Winthrop "acknowledged that he was convinced . . . and would endeavor (by God's assistance) to take up a more strict course hereafter."

The first ten years of the Bay Colony, during which (as during his life, which ended in 1649) Winthrop was generally either governor or deputy governor, were the most difficult years, involving as they did not only matters economic and military and diplomatic, but, above all, theological controversies. Winthrop was not a theologian, yet, in the offices he held, he could not avoid involvement and probably would not have judged it right to do so.

Most painful were the cases of Roger Williams and Anne Hutchinson. There was no real disagreement in his own time that Williams was a kind of saint, as there was no disagreement over his having, when he spoke, a kind of magnetic charm over those who heard him. Both Bradford and Winthrop felt affection for the man whom Cotton Mather, writing at a distance in the *Mag-*

nalia, could see only in terms of his "windmill" gyrations of doctrine. Winthrop conscientiously recognized his affection for the saint and his distrust of the perfectionist and (so far as this world and especially the Colony were concerned) disintegrating doctrines by concurring in his banishment yet privately writing him to steer his course to Narragansett Bay and the Indians—the Indians, to whom (among his other heresies) Williams thought New England belonged, not to English king or Parliament.

Mrs. Hutchinson was a yet harder case, for Sir Henry Vane, at the critical time governor of the Colony, was her adherent; her views purported (not without considerable warrant) to have been derived from her pastor, first in England and then in New England, the Reverend John Cotton, teacher of the Boston Church; and most of the First Church of Boston adhered to her views—the chief and few exceptions being the Reverend John Wilson, pastor [4] of the Boston Church, and Winthrop himself. Winthrop records her trial at length in his *Journal,* first calling her "a woman of ready wit and bold spirit," as indeed she was—and, I may add, one who 'knew her Bible' as well as the clergy. He also wrote *A Short Story of the Rise, Reign, and Ruin of the Antinomians, Familists, and Libertines That Infected the Churches of Massachusetts Bay*, published at London in 1644.

'Antinomian' is the term which, not inappropriately, was applied to Mrs. Hutchinson. Its proof texts are in that great Protestant source book, St. Paul's Epistle to the Romans; and, though the Hutchinsonian terminology somewhat differs, the doctrine is clear enough: she upholds justification by faith as against justification by good works. 'Good works' as such are no proof of salvation; indeed, they are 'good' only so far as they emanate from faith. This is sound enough Pauline doctrine, and even Puritan doctrine: Mrs. Hutchinson's error of strategy was that she could not keep from saying that all the Puritan clergy except Cotton *really* taught salvation by works—comments untactful and probably uncharitable. But her final demolition came when—after months of pressure—she went beyond what, in the next century, Edwards was to say[5] and went behind spiritually prompted interpretation of the Scriptures to the mystical claim of immediate and personal revelation.

Vane was succeeded as governor by Winthrop, re-elected—who had finally to execute the Court's banishment of Mrs. Hutchinson. This action of his so aroused the Boston Church that the governor felt it necessary to explain his position, ending his explanation with a characteristic remark: "He would give them one reason which was a ground for his judgment, and that was: for that he saw that those brethren [the followers of Mrs. Hutchinson and her brother, the Rev. John Wheelwright] were so divided from the rest of the country in their judgment and practise as it could not stand with the public peace that they should continue amongst us. So, by the example of Lot in Abraham's family, and after [the example of] Hagar and Ishmael, he saw they must be sent away."

His "one reason," fortified by Biblical precedents only slightly derogatory, is that dissension in a small community, dissension both in theory and in practice, does not make for peace and order. I add only, from Winthrop's preceding propositions, that he believed in such a theological case—though it had its social consequences—the magistrate should act only, as he had done, by the "advice and direction" of the clergy and according to the oath he had taken upon assuming public office—that he would vote according to his "judgment and conscience." The doublet, so characteristic of Old Testament style, is doubtless not to be subjected to 'close criticism'; if it were, I should need to say that the two criteria are not cognates: one can't use his conscience aright unless that conscience uses the best judgment it can command, that kind of judgment which looks both to relevant precedents in the past and to probable consequences in the future. But this kind of conscience Winthrop, I think, intended.

Opening the *Journal* at random (as men used to open the Bible, that their eyes might fall on a text relevant to their need), I find an entry of 1639, about a woman of whom history has not heard, which has some relevance to the famous cases in which banishment from the Colony was the utmost punishment.

"Dorothy Talby was hanged at Boston for murdering her own daughter, a child of three years old. She had been a member of the church of Salem, and of good esteem for godliness, etc.; but, falling at difference with her husband, through *melancholy or spiritual delusions*, she sometimes attempted to kill him and her children—and herself, by refusing meat, saying *it was so revealed to her. . . .*" She was patiently admonished by the Elders of the church, but, as these measures were of no avail, she was excommunicated. The magistrate caused her to be whipped, and for a time, she seemed saner, "but soon after she was so possessed with Satan that he persuaded her by his delusions—which she listened to as Revelations from God—to break the neck of her own child, that she might free it from future misery. . . ." 'Future' in 1965 would be taken as referring to the pains of this our earthly life; but in 1639 it is more likely to be a reference to eternity. The 'elect' are few; most men are born to a prospect of eternal damnation.

In 1642 Winthrop records briefly another case of what Robert Burton would classify as 'religious melancholy,' that of a Hingham woman "long in a sad melancholic distemper near to frenzy," who several times, though unsuccessfully, tried to drown her three-year-old child. "She could give no other reason for it but that she did it to save it *from misery*, and without that she was assured [certain, I suppose] that she had sinned against the Holy Ghost [—the "unpardonable sin" of Matthew 12:31, which has by its menacing vagueness tormented many generations of Protestants] and that she could not repent of any sin." Winthrop, then governor, makes, as comment on her case, a remark not very emphatic, to be sure, but sensible: "Thus doth Satan work, by the advantage of our infirmities, which should stir us up to cleave the more fast to Christ Jesus and to walk more humbly and watchfully in all our conversation."

There were repeated difficulties with the Plymouth colony over boundaries. But in 1643 four of the New England colonies formed a confederation—primarily, but only primarily—for mutual protection against Indian attacks: the Bay Colony and Plymouth, Connecticut (Hooker's colony at Hartford), and New Haven, leaving out the two colonies of Rhode Island and those Maine settlements of Sir Ferdinando Gorges, because (Winthrop is speaking of the Maine settlements, but his words might be applied to those of Rhode Island as well) "they ran a different course from us, both in their ministry and civil administration."

There were difficulties about the ethics of business—especially what used to be called the 'just price.' In a General Court held at Boston, "great complaint was made of the oppression used in the country in the sale of foreign commodities. . . ." The chief offender, Robert Keayne, was charged with taking above sixpence in the shilling profit, in some cases, above eightpence. The members of the Court thought he should be fined two hundred pounds; the magistrates [the governor and the deputy governor] that he should be fined one hundred. The difference in the penalties proposed was adjusted, doubtless at the instigation of Winthrop, then governor; and the Reverend John Cotton, at his next 'lecture'—the Thursday evening Puritan sermon—addressed himself to the general topic, giving as among "false principles" "that a man might sell as dear as he can and buy as cheap as he can" and among true "rules for trading" that "a man may not sell above the current price, i.e., such a price as is usual in the time and place and as another (who knows the worth of the commodity) would give for it. . . ."

So busy with public concerns was Winthrop—he would have liked to retire from public life at the end of the Colony's first ten years—that through misjudgment of his chief steward he went through something like bankruptcy. But, in his private crisis, the General Court and the freemen of the Colony—an act of public gratitude—saved him. He had nearly ten more years to live, years with new problems—the major, perhaps, being whether in the Commonwealth period he should return to England, which, king and archbishop beheaded, was now going through that same disintegrating toleration, that same combination of perfectionism and splintering, which he had managed to control in New England.

Whatever his motive—or combination of motives—he decided to stay where he was. Doubtless, he considered the matter carefully, with "judgment and conscience."

ROGER WILLIAMS
(1604–83)

Williams, a Londoner, sponsored in his youth by Sir Edward Coke, the jurist, took his degree at Pembroke College, Cambridge, in 1629, and may or may not have been ordained a priest in the Anglican Church; he was at any event by 1629 not only a Puritan but a Separationist. The story of his shifts of doctrinal position is as dazzling as that of Orestes Brownson; and it is not strange that such readiness to embrace a new truth or insight, immediately preach it to others, and then pass on should make him seem lovable but unstable to men like Governors Bradford and Winthrop and, to men like Cotton Mather, a windmill. Unstable, perhaps, but not oscillatory; for his changes were, like Brownson's, in one direction. That general direction was, like Milton's, away from ecclesiasticism and toward spiritual isolation.

Upon his arrival at Boston in 1631, he was invited to become a minister of the First Church, the post later accepted by his archenemy, John Cotton. But the Bay Puritans were not, like the Pilgrims, Separationists. By virtue of an elaborate casuistry, they were what has been called 'Non-Separatist Congregationalists,' who, though they had really broken with the liturgy and ecclesiastical hierarchy of the English Church, denied that they had 'separated' from it. Attached as they were to the parish system, and convinced as they were that they represented the true Reformed English Church with its Reformation carried out in full, not left in a half-way state of compromise, and aware as they were of the many shifts in policy which had taken place since the time of Henry VIII, they were not unadulterated equivocators, but their theories about ordination and the like perilously approached that kind of double-talk or compromise of which Williams would have none.

After a year at Plymouth, within Separatist territory, Williams became minister at Salem. There, along with convincing the Salem women to follow the Pauline injunction to veil their heads in the meetinghouse (I Cor. 11:5–10), Williams acted in more serious matters. He attacked the Bay Charter on the ground that the king of England had no right to the disposal of the land and that the colonists should purchase it from the Indians whose it was. And he attacked the right of the civil magistrates to punish offenses in the First Table—the theological table—of the Ten Commandments. Breach of the Sabbath and taking the oath of loyalty to the commonwealth were sins for the regenerate; and if both regenerate and unregenerate must live together in a community, only the church could deal with the theological offenses. It was a profanation to force them upon the unregenerate, and not the province of the magistrates to do so: theirs was but to punish social offenses like 'false witness,' stealing, and adultery; Williams' 1644 *Queries* sums up civil offenders as "robbers, murderers, tyrants."

For these doctrines, ill-calculated to serve the New England Puritans' reputation in England, and—one may think—for the general nuisance such a perpetual breeder of new doctrines and samples might become, Williams was about to be deported for England by the magistrates when, probably at the warning of Governor Winthrop, he took flight into the country of the Narragansett Indians and became the founder of the Providence Plantation.

Even before his banishment he was suspected of Anabaptist ideas, and after his arrival he was baptized by Holyman, a 'se-baptist,' or self-baptizer. This act, one which substituted adult immersion for infant baptism, the point at issue between Congregationalists and Baptists, but briefly satisfied Williams; for a few months after it, Williams had become a Seeker, one of that large if unorganized group of Englishmen who judged that, since a few years after the Apostles or indeed after the Ascension of Christ, "there *is* no Church, no sacraments, no pastors, no Church officers, no ordinances in the world." Cotton Mather adds, of the Seekers, that they were waiting for the coming of new apostles and meanwhile held to the "principle that every one should have liberty to worship God according to the light of his own conscience, but owning of no churches or ordinances now in the world."

With Williams' aid, Anne Hutchinson and other exiles from the orthodox Puritan communities bought from the Indians in 1638 the island of Aquidneck, with Portsmouth as its center, and two more such colonies were founded before Williams in 1644–45 secured from the English Crown a liberal charter for a united Rhode Island—a charter made yet more liberal upon the Restoration. Williams was governor of Rhode Island, 1654–57, and, during his governership, to the numerous Quaker colonists were added Jews, who settled in Newport. I do not know of any Roman Catholics who came to Rhode Island in the seventeenth century; but, unlike his friend Milton who drew the line at tolerating the intolerant Papists, Williams had no theoretical objection to having them. He saw that Papists are "so partial as to persecute when they sit at the helm and yet cry out against persecution when they are under the hatches," but he saw also that the Puritans of New England did the same: "the righteous judge of the whole world" has only "to present as in a water or glass (where face answers to face) the faces of the Papist to the Protestant, answering to each other in the sameness of partiality"—each persecuting when at the helm, each appealing, when under the hatches, to the principle of toleration.

There is an episode at the end of Williams' life which at first surprises one, then becomes intelligible and even highly honorable. In old age the Apostle of Religious Freedom (as he is often considered) took part in a three-day debate with the Quakers, and in 1676 published two volumes, *George Fox Digg'd out of His Burrows.* In freely permitting the Quakers to live in his colony, so long as they (or Turks or Persians) obeyed the civil laws, Williams, as the debate makes clear, is in no way to be considered as supposing all theologies to be equally true. He did not. He merely denied that false theology could be rectified by the sword, the firebrand, imprisonment, or persecution. Persecution of bodies might make men hypocrites; it could not convince minds. Argument must be met by argument.

Though a Seeker so far as any legitimate Church is concerned, and though (in contradiction to his Puritan brethren) Williams sharply separated the Old and the New Testaments, regarding the former as a history of types which were fulfilled by the *anti-types* of the New, and rejected the Puritan practice of holding the two Testaments as equally valid as sources and proof-texts for doctrine and discipline, he could not follow the early Quakers in dismissing or sliding over the claims to history of the Gospels and in effect denying the Incarnation in order to insist on the mystical birth of Christ in the soul. Nor could he accept their doctrine, freely admitted in Robert Barclay's *Apology*, the sober exposition of the Friends' faith, that Scripture was second to the Inner Light as the source of religious authority.

It is not easy to understand Williams' position, one which—as his best modern interpreter has shown—is not of any current variety. He is a Calvinist and Bible student without being a Presbyterian or Congregationalist. He is a Seeker without being a believer in the Inner Light or 'immediate revelation' or any other kind of mystical epistemology. He is not an advocate of toleration either because of believing there is equal truth in all religions or because of thinking them all equally false or matters of private opinion. It would be accurate to say that he fights for the separation of Church and state if it be understood that he has no belief in 'organized religion' and that he has no Hobbesian belief that the state is, in effect, to take the place of religion. Williams is no secularist, and, so far as 'religion' is concerned, he is some kind of purist for whom the state is a civil compact based upon grounds of some supposed 'natural morality' independent of religious sanctions—a dubious position.

A whimsical, yet also shrewd Puritan, Nathaniel Ward, the 'Simple Cobbler of Aggawam,' asserted: "That state that will give liberty of conscience in matters of religion must give liberty of conscience and conversation in their moral laws . . ."; and, I must say, I find this difficult to deny. That Christian theology and Christian ethics can be separated and the ethics found to be self-evident seems to me a natural Victorian naiveté, for Victorians who had 'lost their religion' had already been reared in it and its ethics. It is not today self-evident.

But Williams' position is yet harder to comprehend. He thinks God's only 'chosen people' were the Jews; and no other people or Church can claim the same relation to God. Yet the Jews are no longer the 'chosen people,' and their book, the Old Testament, is now a book of interest only as it types the anti-types fulfilled in Christ's life, death, and resurrection. Since the Apostles' death, there is no 'valid' nation or Church; there is only the New Testament—as interpreted by Williams.

Such a summary may or may not be true; for, as Perry Miller says, Williams (undeniably, I should think, a saintly man) is more concerned to expose the intellectual errors and the self-righteousness of the 'good' and 'saintly' than he is to exposit—or adumbrate—some perhaps apocalyptic or millennial view of that state for which the Seekers are seeking.

And now we come to that part of Williams' thinking and feeling which has made him remembered—one might at first call it the negative part of his teaching, but it is urged with such force and sweetness that 'negative' seems too negative. Everyone in Williams' time—and many in ours—invoked the claims of the private conscience and inveighed against those seeking to suppress it—or at least its public utterance. But, as we know, it is easy to be tolerant in matters concerning which we have no convictions—the tolerance of indifference. And we know, as Williams did, how those "under the hatches" appeal for toleration, only, when "at the helm," to give good reasons for not tolerating the ones whom they, in turn, have put "under the hatches." Williams belongs to neither of these groups, nor, I think, did his friend Milton. Their appeals for toleration and freedom from censorship were based on hopes not to be borne out by anything in history—'mystical' hopes and faith. One can say that, if unarmed ideas can be left to contend with unarmed ideas, new truth will emerge: not the polemic of forensic truth elicited by partisanship but the truth of quiet, meditative exploration.

For Williams, I think, his famous controversy with Cotton over toleration of conscience is really to be viewed as a needed preliminary. Before men can think freely, we have first to free them from the alternatives of 'conformity' (tacit hypocrisy) or persecution (by death, exile, and suppression and censorship of their writings—their 'life-blood').

Williams and Cotton were men of very different temperaments: Williams, a man who no sooner had an idea than he acted upon it; Cotton, a man of much forethought and afterthought. To his enemies, and even his critics, Cotton seemed a compromiser and a casuist—both in England and in New England. Of his dealings with the archbishop of York, while he was still Puritan rector of St. Botolph's, his recent monographer writes: "Cotton himself was far from hypocritical, but as a veteran of Elizabethan university politics he had learned that when he had a superior inclined to sympathy, the wisest procedure was to agree with him as far as was conscientiously possible, and then to disagree in humble tone, professing always a willingness to cooperate." Williams, on the other hand, had, when they were both still in England, presumed to rebuke Cotton for complying with the Book of Common Prayer.

Cotton was undoubtedly both a scholar and a man of real piety. Both Roger Williams and Anne Hutchinson had good reasons for thinking him either definitely on their sides or at least understanding and sympathetic. Of the New England theologians he was "the least legalistic, the most responsive to allegories and typologies." And when Mrs. Hutchinson was tried before the Assembly, Cotton stood by her, who claimed him as teacher, till she unfortunately offered, of her own accord, statements claiming immediate revelation, not merely new insights given through pondering the text of the Sacred Scriptures. Even after her banishment and death, he continued to preach a doctrine not very different from what stirred Mrs. Hutchinson—the "power of grace and the passivity of the believer. His urgings to await Christ at night, to take heart from the trickling of grace much more than from the flood, to continue wading deeper and deeper into Christ, to feel the divinity welling up inside one, found a more enthralled audience . . . than the words of any of his colleagues."

But Cotton, scholar and man of piety, was also a statesman and something of an administrator. Though he doubtless had some vanity, he was, I think, chiefly concerned that the new-founded Bay Colony should achieve some order and sequence. The Hutchinsons and the Williamses might be tolerated in an already firmly established state; in one but recently planted, and subject to scrutiny by English Presbyterians and Independents and

Quakers and Seekers, some more cautious policy must be pursued. I cannot give proof-texts for this reading of Cotton, and likely none exists, but only such a view accounts for Cotton's career and its end, one unaccompanied by any qualms of conscience. He was not an evil man, though with tendencies toward the 'mystical,' he sought to be cautious, Christianly sensible.

The published controversy between Williams and Cotton was stopped only by the latter's death. As it is, the successive titles constitute an aesthetic delight, only half-pardonable when one considers the seriousness of both of the disputants and their topic. Williams published *The Bloody Tenent of Persecution for Cause of Conscience Discussed* (1644); Cotton, *The Bloody Tenent Washed and Made White in the Blood of the Lamb* (1647); Williams, *The Bloody Tenent Yet More Bloody by Mr. Cotton's Endeavor to Wash It White in the Blood of the Lamb* (1652). Each follows the 'old way' of replying, point by point, to his adversary's arguments (as 'judicious Hooker' in his *Ecclesiastical Polity* did to the contentions of the Puritans). If Williams is the more eloquent, he suffers from the disadvantage of casting his pieces into the form of dialogues between allegorical figures, Peace and Truth, friends both of whom speak Williams' own language. Cotton is the closer and cooler reasoner; Williams, the man of feeling and insight.

Perhaps the center of their argument has to do with their rival interpretations of St. Matthew, the thirteenth chapter. Who are signified by the tares sown by an enemy amid the householder's field of good wheat? According to Cotton these are the hypocrites whom not even pastoral vigilance can keep from entering the visible Church; according to Williams they are the unelect. But Williams, who thinks the world evil and the tares many, stresses the Lord's command to his servants that they are not to try in this world to separate the elect, "lest while ye gather up the tares, ye root up also the wheat with them. Let both grow together until the harvest. . . ."

For Williams, this parable is a warning against over-zealous separatism and segregationalism and state-supported churches and union of Church and state. At some time or other after his departure into the wilderness, Williams came to share the view of St. Paul and Milton and the Quakers, the Seekers, and the Shakers. His *Hireling Ministry None of Christ's* appeared in 1652, when even the English Independents were deciding that tithes should still be collected for the support of the clergy, only the right kind of clergy. Williams' experience of the established Congregational Church of Massachusetts, which supported its clergy by taxes collected from all, and which required all men, whether church members or not, to attend church or be penalized, drove home to him the lesson that one state-supported and monopolistic church was not, in relation to man's conscience, essentially different from another.

For a modern reader the chief issue between Cotton and his adversary lies not in differences in ecclesiastical polity or Scriptural exegesis but in the 'bloody tenet of persecution.' Cotton, like Milton (*Against Prelaty*), seems to assume that St. Paul's Epistles to Timothy and Titus (traditionally the first bishops of Ephesus and Crete), settle the pattern of church government; and to Titus, St. Paul wrote, "A man that is an heretic after the first and second admonition reject, knowing that he is such is subverted and sinneth, being condemned of himself." This serves as the basis for Cotton's chief charge—that those who reject the second presentation of the 'truth' by their pastor are to be excommunicated or exiled or 'persecuted' not for their conscience, thus far presumably ill-informed, but for sinning against their conscience.

Williams never quite bluntly asks how one can distinguish whether a man is suffering for, or sinning against, his conscience, or how another can judge whether a man's conscience is well informed or not. Nor does he ever quite take Milton's position, "Let Truth, neither licensed nor prohibited, and Falsehood grapple; who ever knew Truth put to the worse in a free and open encounter?" He does, however, appeal to history, especially English history, to show how, with theological shifts on the part of the State Church, now one, now another, kind of conscience would be found sinning against itself because disagreeing with established doctrine; and finally he asserts the popular doctrine urged by English Reformers against Rome: "... without search and trial, no man attains this faith and right persuasion. . . . In vain have English Parliaments permitted English Bibles in the poorest English houses, and the simplest man or woman to search the Scriptures, if yet against their souls' persuasion from the Scripture, they should be forced (as if they lived in Spain or Rome itself, without the sight of a Bible) to believe as the church believes."

This simple precept of having every English reader read his Bible for himself has, in justice to Williams, to be accompanied by the reminders that such a reader will have to test his convictions by argument with other Bible readers and that he who gives the precept also believes that no one should be coerced into an interpretation by a shrewd debater.

Along with his distinction between "persecution" for a rightly informed conscience or for a blind and erroneous conscience, Cotton likewise lays down a maxim which sounds sensible and practical and modern indeed:

that "in points of doctrine, some are fundamental, without right belief whereof a man cannot be saved; others are circumstantial . . . , wherein a man may differ in judgment without prejudice of salvation."

Such a proposition as this might suggest to some the principles common to Roman Catholics, Eastern Orthodox, Anglicans, and orthodox Protestants. It does not to Williams, or Cotton, apparently; but Williams is disposed to deny this proposition on the ground that since "the first primitive Christian state or worship" whole generations "have and do err fundamentally concerning the true nature, constitution, gathering, and governing of the Church. And yet far be it from a pious breast to imagine that they are not saved. . . ."

Again, confronted with Cotton's statement, Sir Thomas Browne and the Dryden of *Religio Laici* would plead the case of the virtuous pagans and heathens, the Jews and the Turks. Williams never quite reaches this position, though he respects the American Indians and their faith, though he allows Jews to settle in Rhode Island. Conscience, he writes Governor Endicott, "is found in all mankind, more or less: in Jews, Turks, Papists, Protestants, pagans." I have to fill a gap here. All men, having more or less conscience, can obey the civil law of the state. As for the Church, it has no business to coerce consciences to conformity to Anglo-Saxon and Puritan conformity.

To "batter down idolatry, false worship, heresy, schism, blindness, hardness, out of the soul and spirit, it is vain, improper, and unsuitable to bring those weapons which are used by persecutors—stocks, whips, prisons, swords, gibbets, stakes . . . ; but against these spiritual strongholds in the souls of men, spiritual artillery and weapons are proper."

"Will the Lord Jesus (did He ever in His own person practice, or did He appoint to) join to His breastplate of righteousness the breastplate of iron and steel? ... To His two-edged sword, coming forth of the mouth of Jesus, the material sword, the work of smith's girdle and cutler's?" "Spiritual and soul punishment ... belongs to that spiritual sword with two edges, the soul-piercing (in soul-saving or soul-killing), the word of God."

What Williams thus eloquently preached, he practiced; and, so far from thinking his debate with the Quakers a mark of his senility, I judge it the best evidence that he believed what so eloquently he said. The Quakers were not expelled or punished; they were argued with. Williams was not tolerant of diverse religions on that easy ground of indifference to all but on that solid and spiritual ground of thinking true religion a matter of experiment and experience—something to be arrived at only by the free spirit freely finding its way to the Father of Light.

In his own judgment Williams never grossly sinned against his conscience. Nor could he think that his conscience was less "instructed" than that of John Cotton, any more than Milton thought his less instructed than that of another truly conscientious teacher, Archbishop Laud. It was never quite given to any of these men to assert that equally instructed and mature consciences might come to equally sincere but very different conclusions—in this life. A philosophic theologian or theological philosopher has, I think, to add some such phrase. The truth must be held to be one, though some men see a part of it and others another part. We are like the blind men who described the elephant in terms of the parts they touched: all they reported was true, as fragments are true.

Williams' defense of religious toleration was not disinterested in the sense of being motiveless or being without initial personal motivation. He himself had, as he believed, been persecuted for obeying his conscience. But his establishment of a tolerating colony and his written attacks on the "bloody tenet" are not to be disposed of because they were not ultrasupernaturally disinterested. His own case opened out into a far from merely personal one. Rash, Utopian, prophetically millennial, he raised the whole issue of conscience in relation to vested authority.

Contemporary historians of ideas see that he has, by contemporary liberals, been wrested from his historical context and translated into modern secularist terms alien to his deeply religious spirit. But there is danger, too—more heinous, I think—in confining great spirits to their historical context, that context which, by constant implication, they transcend.

MICHAEL WIGGLESWORTH
(1631–1705)

Wigglesworth has long been known as the author of *The Day of Doom* (1662), an immensely popular presentation of Judgment Day written in ballad meter, with abundant rhyme to aid the memory. The 'poet' and pastor of Malden, Massachusetts, sickly most of his life and from 1663 to 1685 too ill to preach, nonetheless lived into his seventy-fourth year; for his last twenty years he was remarkably restored to life and, though (as one of the Mathers called him in the obituary sermon) "a little feeble shadow of a man," preached two or three times a week; he also continued the practice of medicine, to the learning and application of which he had applied himself during the more than twenty years when he was too ill to preach, and was, in general, more active than at any earlier period of his valetudinarian life.

His recently published "Diary" covers but the years from February 1653 to May 1657, the period during which he was tutor and fellow at Harvard and attempting to make up his mind which parish to choose to serve, and whether to marry or not. It ends, approximately, with the first of his three marriages and the acceptance of the pastorate of Malden.

The "Diary" is a document of much interest, and happily (if one can use that word of a sustained self-analysis of sin, doubt, and hesitation) covers the author's formative years—"la jeunesse de," as French literary scholars call a monograph which limits itself to the period of choosing a vocation—the period before one publishes his first successful book and becomes a more or less public character.

Wigglesworth hasn't the "effusive facility" of Cotton Mather, and, not having it, he can make relatively clear and specific what his particular sins were. He has none of Mather's 'mystic' or manic states. He has a 'bad conscience,' a sense of guilt, pretty persistently, and no angels to reassure him of the high destiny which, even in this life, is to be his. His is an abundance of fears and scruples.

By temperament, apparently, he is a 'high-strung' and tense young man. The two patent examples have to do with the banging of doors—eruptive sounds which probably got on his nerves. One Sabbath eve and the following day he hears the stable doors of the Reverend W. Mitchell "beat to and fro with the wind." Not many days thereafter he hears the doors of a nearby house "blow to and fro with the wind in some danger to break, as I think. . . ." The irritations caused by these irregular sounds distract him from his study and vex his "poor, fainting, decaying body," but he has, centrally, to translate his irritation into concern for others and the well-being of *their* property: the question "whether I should, *out of duty,* shut it [the stable door] or not"; and he adds, what is doubtless quite honest, "no temptations perplex me so sorely as such like *when I am not clear concerning my duty . . . I cannot tell* whether it were my duty."

Perhaps it is first in Wigglesworth's "Diary" that I meet these two characteristics of what, at least by the nineteenth century, came to be recognized as the 'New England conscience': first, in everything, the presence of a *duty* to be performed, and second, with a further turn of the moral screw, the anxious uncertainty what that duty is.

Wigglesworth took great pleasure—even if an anxious one—in his secular studies and his work as tutor in Hebrew. But deeply drilled into him is the most rigorous kind of doctrine that reading the Bible is more important than humanistic study—still more, that one ought not to feel any *natural human* pleasure either in the performance of one's work or any *natural human liking* for one's students and friends. God alone is to be loved, and other people one is to treat impersonally because God has told us that we should "love them as ourselves." Wigglesworth never cites Scripture text or theologian, but he seems to have been reared, or to have reared himself, in the rigid view not only that we should have no 'personal friends' but that any spontaneous preferences among God's creatures deprive God of the total loyalty which should be His.

'Interested in his students' as, in the language of twentieth-century 'educators,' Wigglesworth unquestionably was, he is sensitive to how they respond to him—even identifying himself with the Hebrew which he teaches and so regarding their absence of interest in it as a slight on him. He appears to have felt no 'unnatural' attraction to the young men whom he, also young, though a little older, taught; but that he should particularly be drawn to some of them and that he should have what would now be called 'pride in his work' both seem to him sinful. There is, again, a curious anticipation of later New England in his feeling that *duty* and *pleasure* must be in necessary opposition, particularly, indeed, in the feeling that my *duty*, if I do it with *pleasure*, must have in it—whether or no I can define it—something sinful. "I feel a need of Christ's blood to wash me from the *sin of my best duties*. . . . I find my heart prone to take secret pleasure in thinking how much I do for others' good, but, Lord, how little of it is done for Thee. I fear there is much sensuality and *doting upon the creature* in my pursuit of the good of others; I cannot seek God's glory therein, but am carried [motivated most] *with pity to man*." "I find my spirit so exceeding carried with love to my pupils that I can't tell how to take up my rest in God."

The young tutor makes himself attend sermons and 'lectures' (midweek sermons) and read the Bible, but he is bored, distracted, wishes he were free to pursue his studies. "I cannot prevail against that cursed frame to think the time long that I spend in reading God's Word. Pride—and sensual affection's outgoings of heart after my studies—again get head." "I cannot but hanker after my studies whilst I am reading God's Word. . . ." He tires of hearing sermons and 'lectures' given by others.

He records all kinds of intellectual doubts about the truth of the Christian theology he has been taught—doubts which he subsumes under the general name of atheism. For examples he has doubts (too numerous and in kind too various to cite) concerning the sacrament of the Lord's Supper. "I find that the clearest *arguments* that can be cannot persuade my heart to believe the being of a god, if God do not let the beams of his glory shine into it"—which appears to mean that intellectual arguments for the existence of God mean nothing to him unless his own *heart* is moved. He is assaulted by doubts of the accuracy of the text of Scripture: doubts "whether every word of the Scriptures were *infallible* because of the possibility of mistakes in the writings [inaccurate transcription] and because of the points in the Hebrew [which indicate what vowels are to be inserted between the consonants: were these *points* of Divine origin?] and the various readings in the text and margin." He is puzzled whether the Gospels of Mark and Luke have "divine authority" though their authors were not apostles.

Rather rebellion than intellectual doubt is Wigglesworth's choicest specimen of his own temporary 'atheism.' He has been taught contemplative doctrines of God and the 'future life' which he, frail in body but *activist* of spirit, finds repellent: "I cannot desire heaven because 'tis a place where I shall see, and wonder at, and acknowledge, the glory of God, forever. *But I rather* desire a Heaven where I might be *doing* for God than only thinking and gazing on His excellency."

Again returns this stark opposition of love of God and love of one's neighbor. The Bible—even the New Testament—can be quoted in textual proof of almost any reasonable position. It is true that "God needs no service of mine"—"no one is indispensable" in the gross professional sense. But God has sent every man into the world with something which he, uniquely, can do: God has sent every man into the world with a *vocation*, a 'calling'—and "Woe is me if I preach not the Gospel" I was sent into the world to preach.

In the extreme Puritan emphasis on man's *irrelevance* to God and man's duty to want to *do* good as well as be godly (doctrines which most sensible Puritans could take with the proper seasoning of salt), and again on man's duty to glorify God and to tolerate other men only because Christ has given us a Second Commandment—in all this Wigglesworth has no doubt of its truth, but he, not dishonorably, rebels and honestly records his rebellion: "My actions are all so full . . . of *seeking the creature*, or to have others happy and myself comforted in others' happiness [and I feel] so much weariness in *holy duties* [the last phrase he elsewhere paraphrases as "the public ordinances"—the "feared length" of the sermons, and so on]." But St. John says in his First Epistle, "He who loveth not his brother whom he *hath* seen, how can he love God, whom he hath *not* seen?" I am content to believe that there are some souls (by her own testimony, Evelyn Underhill was one, and Jonathan Edwards was assuredly another) who start from the Absolute (as the Hindus say, God without shape), with what Edwards philosophically translates love to God into—"benevolence to Being in general": "True virtue must chiefly consist in love to God, . . . that being who has the greatest share of universal existence." But the Hindus tolerantly allow also the worship of God 'with shape.'

One 'natural affection' Wigglesworth allowed as proper and no derogation from the glory of God or "doctrine upon the creature." But, alas, he could not give himself a good grade in this category, that of (according to Protestant numbering) the Fifth Commandment,—filial duty towards father and mother. His father, early lamed and relatively poor, apparently 'made sacrifices' to send his son to Harvard; yet Wigglesworth, returning home, from his Harvard fellowship, is embarrassed by his father's criticism of him in matters of money and practical judgment generally. He feels he lacks "natural affection and pity" to his "afflicted parents." In the same year, 1653, his father died, and when the news reaches him he feels guilty and tries to confess to God his guilt for "my not prizing them and their life which God has graciously continued so long." A few days later, and subsequently, he has to pray "that I might not be secretly glad that my father was gone."

My impression is that he, who had become a Fellow of Harvard and a young man of promise, was embarrassed by, ashamed of, his parents. Once he is able to generalize, rather too sweepingly, what is involved: his feeling of rebellion against all who are in a position to point out his faults. He is thinking, as so often, of the lack of respect and obstinacy some of his pupils show "in refusing to read Hebrew"; and then he can see the analogy between their behavior and attitude and his own—his own "perverseness" to both his "natural parents and academical" (his own teachers). His own attitude and that of his pupils are symptomatic of a "spirit and unbridled licentiousness"—of insubordination. "Lord, in mercy heal, or *I know not what will become of New England.*" If the New England salt, the only pure and unadulterated salt, has lost its savor, wherewith, indeed, shall it be salted?

Wigglesworth thought his two chief sins to be "carnal lusts" and pride. Both "carnal" and "lust"—at least when not conjoined—had for a seventeenth-century Puritan a much wider meaning than today. "Lust" often simply means "desire," and when, during the latter period of the journal, Wigglesworth is busy 'candidating' in search of a pastoral appointment, he writes "moreover I cannot seek after future settlement [over a parish] without *carnal* aims," he seems to mean little more than that, not having independent means, he has to think as well of the financial as of the purely spiritual aspect of the parochial ministry.

It is clear, however, that the problem of sex troubled him. He records, in shorthand entries, his 'wet dreams' ("some filthiness escaped me in a filthy dream"), and when he speaks of "carnal lusts" he does speak of his shame at these dreams (possibly of his favorite students) as "provocation unto the ejection of seed." "I find myself unable to read anything to inform me about my *distemper* because of the prevailing or rising of my lusts. *This I have procured to myself.*" All of this, and the following entries on the subject, are obscure. There is nothing to indicate that the young man ever had premarital sexual intercourse, either with a young man or with a woman, though conceivably he may, in his heart, have lusted after one of his students, one of those pupils for whom he felt "too much doting affection." Conceivably, he may have practiced masturbation, though his references are always to "filthy thoughts" which come in his dreams. Above all, the modern reader should take warning against reading his frequent adjectives "whoring" and "whorish" ("my whorish departures of heart from the Lord") either literally or in any connection with sex. They occur always in contexts which make clear that they refer to what the Hebrew prophets used to rebuke their people for—the "whoring after false gods"; and the word "whoring" is for Wigglesworth the key word to express absence—or inacceptably little —of love of God.

Wigglesworth decided to marry—the customary and expected thing for a Puritan clergyman to do. Romantic attachment did not enter into this any more than in the case of George Herbert, not a Puritan, who, having decided to become a country parson, thought marriage a safeguard against romanticism. In Wigglesworth's case, there was patently another consideration. As St. Paul, himself a celibate, said bluntly, "Better to marry than to burn." And Wigglesworth had, not like St. Paul, "a thorn in the flesh" (Cotton Mather collected authorities to prove that it was the recurrence of severe headaches), but many: he was always ailing, of many obscure maladies—largely, it would seem, psychosomatic. Among other maladies, however, he did think he had a phallic "distemper" (gonorrhea, he seems, mistakenly, to have thought it), and he wonders whether to marry or take physic "or both." Having discussed the question with physicians, he takes the advice that he should marry, and that, quite speedily, he does. The outcome is too complicated to summarize, except to say that the young man, now minister of Malden, continues to be troubled by colds, catarrh, "spleen," indigestion. His wife (of whom we get no least notion) bears him a child, and he mentions her travail, but dilates on his own discomfort: his sleep broken off, he lay "sighing, sweating, praying, almost fainting through weariness before morning."

The "Diary" ends with his sexual and marital difficulties as he settles at Malden; but I must not forget his sin of pride, which, appropriately, manifests itself in his account of his Harvard tutorship. He finds his actions "all so full of self-seeking, self-exalting and admiring." When he preaches well and is commended, he feels pride. When he teaches well—and argues so well that his arguments find "acceptation with the seniors (though contrary to their former apprehensions)," pride overpowers him. "This week I studied Natural philosophy with Sir Ambrose junior. I found the Lord so extraordinarily assisting me above and beyond my own folly in quickness of invention and reasoning that, instead of admiring my God, I found myself very prone to admire myself. . . ."

Our cleric is sometimes aware of having "distracting scruples of conscience," but his scrupulosity is probably the sin he is least aware of; perhaps he is, indeed, scarcely aware of its being a sin—a form of pride. It is, I suppose, exactly Wigglesworth's scrupulosity which is a part of his interest: it is partly disease, partly sin—as scrupulosity always is: it belongs to that border land between the province of the psychiatrist and that of the moral philosopher or the theologian. It is, one may call it, ethical neuroticism or neurotic moralism—which term shall be substantive and which adjective being a matter of degree. It can always defend itself as rigorism and perfectionism, as the result of setting itself higher standards than those of ordinary Christians. It can always claim to be making those subtle distinctions and discriminations which never occur to the mind of a matter of fact, insensitive 'good man.' And these self-defenses can never be wholly dismissed. All one can finally say is: a morality of self-analysis which ends in intellectual incoherence, wastefully indecisive action, and intellectual and moral pride cannot, at the last, even before the tribunal of its own judgment, claim to be so wonderfully Christian.

COTTON MATHER
(1663–1728)

In Mather we see the combination of tremendous activity (his motto was *fructuous:* fruitful) with fastings (private fastings, for the seventeenth century had public fast days as well), *vigils* (the night spent in prayer and meditation), and *visions* and *auditions*. He lived under a constant strain, both that of activity (surely no man was more intent on doing good and no man more easily confused that with his own importance, so that—as with the family of John Adams—attack on him, difference of judgment from him, was attack on God) and that of passivity, of endeavoring to lead an inward, even a mystical, life.

Mather's 'conscience' is indeed complex, and complex to discuss. He represents neither the assured good conscience of the emigrant Puritans nor the constantly troubled conscience of their descendants. Today, he would probably be dismissed as highly neurotic: as feeling himself ever the object of attention, and as swinging between exalted states, induced both by early and long adulation by some, and depressions and feelings of persecution which grew more frequent as he and his better-balanced father ceased to represent the 'spirit of the age.'

His *Diary*, however, makes it abundantly clear that the two things for which Mather is now chiefly remembered, his part in the Salem witchcraft trials (a part he never, like Samuel Sewall, recanted) and his espousal of vaccination for smallpox (an espousal in which he had the backing of but one of the Boston physicians)—these two things which from a conventionally modern point of view somewhat cancel each other out—were both but episodes in a *busy* life and scarcely touch him at center.

His *Spiritual Diary* was, as sentences in it make clear, written, if not for publication, at least for the edification of his sons and daughters. After a fashion, he edited his manuscript—not published till 1911—but it is doubtful that unedited it would be very different. He writes in Latin a paragraph so that his first wife, who lived with him and bore him children for sixteen years, shall not be able to read it, but it is puzzling to know why, since in its import—one which has nothing to do with their marital relations—it is not different in kind—indeed, far milder in its declaration of his privileged position with the Almighty—than many passages left in English.

In journalizing his ecclesiastical, moral, intellectual, and religious life, Mather was conscious of following a hallowed Puritan custom. Of Harvard's President Chauncy, he writes in the *Magnalia*, he "kept a diary, the loss of which I cannot but mention with regret: nevertheless I can report this much of it, that it was *methodized* under the heads of *sins* and *mercies*"—a method which Mather from time to time follows. *Mercies* are the things one has to be thankful for, like a large congregation and—what Mather never fails to mention—a large library (one which, even before he was forty, included between two and three thousand volumes). In the *Magnalia* the diaries and the like are often called the "private" or "reserved" writings.

The two strongest impressions made by the *Spiritual Diary* are at opposite poles. Dr. Franklin shrewdly seized upon and praised *one* side of Mather—his intense desire to be publicly, actively, industrious in promoting any and all manner of what he deems good causes—this almost invariably coupled with the desire to have his 'essays to do good' published—preferably in London, but if not in Boston. He writes a book to convert the Indians; he learns Spanish in order to compose a book to convert Spanish-reading people to Protestantism; he adapts a catechism for children; he writes giving advice to young men how to be and remain good while young (having already 'organized' groups of young men, precursive, perhaps, of the innumerable organized groups of young men attached to each sect).

The other side of him is 'ascetic' and 'mystical': I use both these words in quotes. It is a commonplace to say of mystics like St. Teresa of Avila that they were both visionaries and administrators; that is, those whose inner life is one of 'unitive prayer,' who are—fed by their communion with the Incarnate Infinite—the truly, the purposefully, active. Mather is a kind of strange Protestant caricature of such a *schema*. I have no notion whether he had read 'the mystics' or not: there is no evidence that he had. But he felt and found his way to some adumbration of theirs—chiefly, it seems, through his reading in the Talmud and the Greek and Latin Fathers, the 'Patristic' writers.

The Puritans practiced public fast days as signs of humiliation and entreaty; but Mather, from his youth, practiced also days of private, of secret, fastings (by which I understand days of going entirely without food, and letting this ascetic practice be known to none save his own household). In the *Magnalia*, writing of his closest personal friend, Thomas Shepard, grandson of the celebrated pastor of the church at Cambridge, he cites his friend's "secret-fasts"—at least once a month and speaks of "the commendations given to fasting by [Sts.] Basil and Cyprian in their orating about it and by [St.] Ambrose in his book of Elias [Elijah]" and says that Shepard's "holy heart could subscribe unto the words of [St.] Chrysostom concerning this duty."

In the *Spiritual Diary*, Mather constantly recurs to accounts of his secret fasts and to comments on the practice among pious Jews and primitive Christians. "The Jews tell us of Rabbi Joshua ben Ananiah that his face was black by reason of his fastings. Why is his name called Ashur (I Chron. 4:5)? Because his face was black by fastings." "Fastings were so frequent among the Christians in the primitive times that it was to be discovered in their *joints* and *faces: pallidi* and *trepidi* were the opprobrious names which for this reason the heathen gave unto them."

In 1702, in his fortieth year, he began to keep vigils —that is, from time to time to spend a "good part of the night" in prayer. "I dismissed my dear consort unto her own repose; and, in the dead of the night, I retired into my own study; and there, casting myself into the dust, prostrate on my study-floor, before the Lord, I was rewarded with communications from Heaven that cannot be uttered.... If these be vigils, I must (as far as the Sixth Commandment ["Thou shalt not kill"—even thyself]) have more of them!"

He records later (1716) having had "many thoughts about writing a book of [on] the Christian Ascetics. My experience therein has been of so great variety that I may do well to consider what *account* should be given of the *talents*."

Long before he begins his vigils, he has on his days of secret fastings something like mystical experiences. He has intense belief in angelic powers, and they constantly appear to him when he prays and bring him assurances of his salvation and of the important work for which God has destined him. Like pious Catholics he even believes he has an especial guardian angel. Often the communications they make "cannot be uttered"—presumably meaning it would be presumptuous of him to record them. But often he does record them. In his twenty-third year he wrote above the entry, "Cum relego, scripsisse pudet!" And, then in Latin also, he records that an angel has appeared to him, asserting that he has been sent by the Lord Jesus. "Many things this Angel said which it is not fit [presumably because they were so flattering] to be set down here." But set down he does the Angel's declaration "that the fate of this youth should be to find full expression for what in him was best; and this he said in the words of the Prophet Ezekiel [Ezek. 31: 3, 4, 5, 7, and 9].... And in particular the Angel spoke of the influence his branches should have, and of the books this youth should write and publish, *not only in America but in Europe*. And he added certain special prophecies of the great works this youth should do for the revolutions that are now in hand. *Lord Jesus, what is the meaning of this marvel?* From the wiles of the Devil, I beseech thee, deliver and defend Thy most unworthy servant."

The concluding prayer shows that Mather was capable of supposing that a devil had assumed angelic form in order to beguile and confuse him, in order to minister to his pride and so undo him—an assumption Scriptural enough. But such fear is, one must confess, rare in Mather. He had a lifelong conviction of the conversion of Europe and England to Puritan Protestantism and that he—all unworthy though he might be—should by his writings be an important instrument in bringing it about.

This kind of conviction in the excessive forms in which Mather understood it has proved illusory. But it seems that, for the most part, men—whether artists, ecclesiastics, or what not—cannot exert their full powers without a degree of belief in their unique importance, which partakes almost always in a degree of illusion. The fact is that Mather felt sustained by the mixture of truth and illusion in his sense of angelic (which amounts to Divine) guidance and that without it he could not have been as unrelentingly active for the causes he believed in as he was.

And this brings me to the consideration of his 'conscience'—by which I mean at once the guide and the judge of a man's moral and religious life. Mather was an immensely learned man and, according to his lights, a good man, but he strikes one as almost totally deficient in conscience as theoretically educative and deficient in a real, as distinct from a ritual and theological, sense of being sinful—either in general (original sin) or in particular (specific sins).

Early in his *Diary* he condemns himself—rightly, no doubt—for "my applauding of myself in my thoughts when I have done anything at all significant: prayed or preached with *enlargements;* answered a question readily, presently, suitably, and the like. *Proud thoughts fly-blow my best performances.*" He notes pride as an especial sin of "young preachers." He charges himself with a "strange unaffectedness of heart when thinking and speaking about the things of God. *Methinks I am but a very parrot in religion.*"

That he is proud Mather ritually admits; that he is vain—much concerned that other men should admire him—he less rarely notes. But in his twenty-third year, before his ordination as his father's coadjutor at the Second Church, he does write: "Our congregation happening this afternoon to be thinner than ordinary, my heart began to sink under some foolish discouragements hereupon"; and he writes down at some length how he vanquished these thoughts, not wholly in that vanity of his counterstatements: "Since I have heretofor had the temptation of being flocked after, let me now suspect that I need a rod . . . and especially be careful to apprehend that an affectation of displaying one's gifts before throngs is too often an abominably proud fishing for popular applause. . . ." Doubtless, he includes *vanity* under the general head of *pride.*

His mind is constantly with thoughts of publishing. That vanity is *mixed* in this desire I think he never sees; for his much writing proves his *industry*, and *sloth* is a sin he frequently reprehends himself for, though I should think he was not to be accused of it even by unfriendly critics; and, of course, his publications, even though they bear his name and spread his fame abroad, are all directed at promoting some especial good cause—good as he sees it. Conscience is his guide more than his judge; and he is more intent on following the light he has had than in doubting whether his light be not partly darkness.

Examination of conscience seems for him to have concerned itself little with his attitudes and behaviors toward his family. It is not till after they had been married for more than fifteen years that he gives thanks (in his record of a "secret thanksgiving" in his study) for his first wife, "dearest consort," and she is then praised in terms which are sufficiently vague: "Her piety, the agreeable charms of her person, her obliging deportment unto me, her discretion in ordering my and her affairs . . . and the lovely offspring that I have received by her . . ."

It is to be assumed that, like Mrs. Jonathan Edwards, she took care of all things temporal; but the picture of the household one can even infer from the *Diary* is strangely dim. Mrs. Mather apparently bore a child nearly every year. Some, naturally, died in infancy, and Mather records the inscriptions he wrote for their graves. Before he had a son, whom he named after his ever-revered and never envied father, he had three little girls, who are mentioned in connection with their clothes catching fire. One little girl's "headgear" caught fire because she got too near the candle. Where was Mrs. Mather when these accidents occurred, and where was the servant or servants? (Mather had a Negro slave whom, with Scriptural appropriateness, he named Onesimus.)

The characteristic episode is that concerning little Katy. As she went into the cellar with a candle, "her muslin ornaments about her shoulders took fire from it and so blazed up as to set her headgear likewise on fire." "Her shriek for help was heard; and the child's life was saved though her neck and hand were horribly burnt." This disaster, coming to his eldest daughter soon after his youngest had suffered an accident of like nature, threw Mather, as he writes, "into extreme distress." But it seems not to have occurred to him or even to Mrs. Mather to have warned the children or taken any other practical measures. Instead, Mather turned this to symbolic edification. When the second accident occurred he laid aside the discourse he had written for delivery at a private gathering of the pious and did, "with much influence from Heaven on my mind, at the sudden compose and utter unto the meeting a discourse for above an hour from Lamentations, 5:13 ['they took the young men to grind, and the children fell under the wood']—the theme being: "What use ought parents to make of disasters befalling their children?" Not even this was the final use of Katy's accident, for on the following Sunday he preached in the Second Church, inciting parents to do their duty to assist in the "salvation of their children" from the fire of the wrath of God.

This emblematizing, as it may be called, is eminently characteristic of Mather—this rather gross seeing of what Swedenborg calls 'correspondences,' the turning of a literal image of a physical property into a spiritual correspondent which, however, is itself not too remote from the physical image which suggested it.

And now I must say something about the whole texture of Mather's spiritual life. He uses all sorts of ritual phrases about what a vile sinner he is. They scarcely ring true; that is why, reluctantly, I call them ritual, for I take it for granted that man is a psychosomatic creature, a soul in a body, and that 'pure' spirituality is a myth. When I speak of 'ritual' I mean, therefore, 'mere' ritual, or ritual in which the balance between the act or phrase and the attitude signified is disproportionately inclined toward the act or phrase rather than the attitude.

Mather's favorite ritual phrase is to describe himself, during his private orisons, as "prostrate in the dust upon my study-floor"—or in more intense states, "I cast myself prostrate on my study-floor with my mouth in the dust." Here, I can't but feel the literal and the ritually symbolic are so intermingled that they defy separation. I suppose he lay prone, but I can't believe the New England dust to be anything except symbolic, and as to the mouth I give up.

And this brings up the larger and extraordinarily difficult question: how does one know whether a man is sincere or not when he uses ritual phrases? One is inclined to feel that some confession of guilt said in one's own idiom is more sincere. But if I say that, I fall into a restatement of the Puritan attack on liturgy and 'set forms' of prayer—while I know well that the attackers developed their own forms, not less susceptible of being 'ritually' said by the clergy and 'ritually' responded to by the congregation. And then if I make the test the confessing of sins in one's own idiom, I am in danger of falling into another trap: that of a man—literary, let us say—who is proud of his powers of discrimination and expression.

Two tests seem somewhat surer. The confession of specific sins seems more likely to be sincere than some blanket indictment of oneself—ultimately, perhaps, a version of the doctrine of 'original sin,' so that one in effect says "I'm a sinner; aren't we all?" or some histrionically exaggerated view of this which, enabling one to speak of himself as "the chief of sinners," plunges one into what may well be another form of pride. And then the world rightly refuses, I think, to make any judgment of sincere penitence which is confession, whether ritual or literary or histrionic: it is how a man subsequently behaves and lives which shows whether he has sincerely repented and not only momentarily thinks of, but now "leads a new life."

I see no signs that Mather's conscience accused him of guilt for his part in the witchcraft trials, and here the *Spiritual Diary* is certainly of assistance in acquitting him either of hypocrisy or of cowardice in making no such recantation as did his friend Judge Sewall, for it is clear that Mather's mind was coherent in its well-nigh thoroughgoing supernaturalism. This belief in Satanic powers was of a piece with a belief in their counterpart and counterpoise—angelic powers. And as a firm believer in God's final triumph in history, he held, not without basis in the Book of Revelation and elsewhere in Scripture, that, as the end of time drew near, Satan would redouble his efforts to thwart the men of God, the establishment of the Holy State, and the final millennium.

It is in accordance with what, despite his immense learning, was a *simple* faith that Mather also believed, even more thoroughgoingly than early Puritans like Governor Winthrop, in Special Providences. Everything in this life has its meaning, ultimately with regard to our eternal destiny. Oft repeated in the *Diary* is his question, "*What does this mean?*" That every least event has a meaning, even a meaning ultimately supernatural, he does not doubt. The question is only one of correct interpretation.

Of prayer, Mather mostly thinks as he does of the fulfillment of prophecies, in simple terms. Doubtless, he subscribed in general to the doctrine that some of our prayers are negatively answered by Divine denial. And occasionally—but not by temperament or habitual mode of thought—he rose beyond 'petitionary prayer' to prayer as an act or attitude of submission to God and union with Him.

JONATHAN EDWARDS
(1703–58)

The name of Edwards is that of a New England saint never to be mentioned without awe and reverence. No man can disinterestedly contemplate Edwards' life and attend closely to his thinking without some incitation to disciplining himself and, as old 'spiritual' writers call it, *recollecting* himself. As Edwards will not allow sentimentality or religiosity to pass for religion, so he will not allow what a philosopher friend of mine used to call "*loose literary* thinking"; he insists in all thinking, whether about the habits of flying spiders or the *Nature of True Virtue*, that it be in clearly defined terms and logically reasoned either from empirical data or from a priori 'first principles.' Reading Edwards is an excellent astringent for literary men. Not only does he permit himself no 'poetic' passages, he is not even, like Berkeley and Hume, an 'elegant' writer. He is as solidly built and stark as a New England meeting house.

The first two documents of his which concern us are his "Resolutions," written down in 1722–23, when he was approximately twenty and was minister of a Presbyterian church on Long Island; and the "Diary," which begins where the "Resolutions" leaves off: it chiefly dates from 1723–25, just before and during his tutorship at Yale; but the last six entries were written (1726–35) after he had become colleague of his grandfather Stoddard at the church in Northampton.

The 'resolutions' are 'rules of life,' to be reread once a week, and they and the "Diary" show the rigorous standards, the discipline, of body, intellect, private and social ethics, and spirituality at which Edwards aimed. They are military, Spartan, Jesuit, Puritan. Not the least interesting aspect of them is the way some of them overlap the disciplines Franklin set himself early in life, and the way in which, incorporated as they are into a metaphysical and Christian system, those seemingly most alike differ when placed in their context. As the history of the Quakers and the early Methodists shows, there are some rules which, though meant for religious ends, are profitable for the life which now is—that of farmers and merchants. Rise early, waste no time, be careful of your diet. The "Diary" entry on diet is perhaps closest to Franklin:

"By a sparingness in diet and eating,—as much as may be [possible]—what is light and easy of digestion, I shall doubtless be able to *think more clearly* and *gain time . . .*"

He repeatedly warns himself against states of indolence; and it is doubtless in these warnings that one finds best the specific meaning in the most ambiguous of his

"Resolutions": "To live with all my might while I do live." For Edwards, a contemplative, "to live" is always to be conscious, intellectually alert, the attention concentrated, the bow always taut. The contrary state he most commonly calls *listlessness*. He recognizes that there are times when one cannot be contemplatively active in any high degree. But at such times one must think what he can do in order not to be idle or *effortless:* Thus: "When I am unfit for other business, to perfect myself in writing characters" (this, I think, means shorthand). Or again, if just the "good" (the centrally challenging) books are lacking to one, he can go over previous acquisitions—"spend time in studying mathematics and in *reviewing* other kinds of old [that is, formerly acquired] learning. . . ." Another therapy, for listlessness: "I am apt to think it a good way, when I am indisposed [feel no eagerness for] reading and study to read of my own remarks, the fruit of my study into divinity, etc., to *set me going again.*" Any systematic intellectual worker will recognize these are practical aids to 'redeeming the time.' When too tired or too distracted to compose, read and take notes; copy out passages into your commonplace book; work at bibliography or indexing.

The concept of *duty* is prominent; and Edwards recognizes that there is no aspect of life morally indifferent. An amusing instance is an early entry from the "Diary," "Have lately erred, in not allowing time enough for *conversation.*" By the word he doubtless meant talk, innocent but 'small' talk—a talent at which he never acquired much skill. But it has its proportionate, if peripheral, importance in the ethical life of a man living in society and in a family.

'Duty' is a basic word-concept in both "Resolutions"

and "Diary." In latter-day New England, Duty ("stern daughter of the voice of God") has become an ethical mandate virtually autonomous; but for Edwards it is still religious as well as ethical: its 'shalls' and 'shall nots' refer to both Tables of the Law. Duty is the giving to all levels of created and creative life their due—what is, hierarchically, owed them. "Render unto Caesar the things which are Caesar's and unto God the things which are God's," Jesus, half casuistically, said to his Jewish inquirers concerning the payment of taxes to Roman political authority. But a philosophical theologian like Edwards has, of course, to recognize that political and ethical duties are ultimately defensive only as types, shadows, and surrogates for the duty due God, the Order in whom all varyingly lesser degrees of duty find their justification. The 'resolution' which makes this clearest and which should, I think, be applied as a 'gloss' to those less clear is no. 62: "*Resolved*, Never to do anything but my duty, and then according to Ephesians VI, 6–8, to do it willingly and cheerfully, *as unto the Lord and not to man* . . . ," that is, never to do anything contrary to "my duty." The concept of action "over and beyond the call of duty" does not occur to Edwards because it, too, comes within the sphere of "my duty." No. 57: "When I fear misfortunes and adversity, to examine *whether* I have done my duty, and resolve to *do* it, and let the event be just as Providence orders it. I will, as far as I can, be concerned about nothing but *my duty*, and *my sin*." Between *duty* and *sin* there is no middle ground of things indifferent, no neutral territory.

The last cluster of injunctions which I wish to note concern what might be called 'Christian Stoicism,' the discipline imposed by the mind and spirit of man upon his *physical* and *emotional* states. "Resolved, to act with sweetness and benevolence . . . in all bodily dispositions, —sick or well, at ease or in pain, sleepy or watchful, and *not to suffer discomposure of my body* to discompose my mind." "Resolved, never to allow any pleasure or pain, joy or sorrow, nor any *affection at all*, nor any degree of *affection* . . . but what helps Religion." 'Affection' will be seen as the term inclusive of the two antonymic pairs named just before it; it would be called now 'feeling' or 'emotion' or (in some technical contexts) 'affect.'

The last 'resolution' which should be cited, written in 1723, reads: "*Resolved*, Constantly, with utmost *niceness* and diligence, and the *strictest scrutiny*, to be looking into the state of my soul, that I may know whether I have *truly* an *interest in Christ* or not. . . ." It would have been surprising had Edwards not resolved to follow the practice of the Puritan saints in England and New England—that of self-examination, whether written in journals or mentally performed at bedtime—the Protestant confessional, as we might call it. The distinctively Edwardsean notes are in "niceness" (precision, exactness) and "strictest scrutiny." These might seem to indicate—what is likely true—that most men's self-examination is relatively self-indulgent. But the opposite may be true. The true direction of these directions is, I think, that—difficult as it is to be objective about the subjective—one should strive for the same objectivity and unaffective precision in self-analysis as when one writes about the habits of flying spiders or the nature of 'disinterested benevolence.'

It is this kind of laboratory objectivity which Edwards shows in his masterpiece, the *Treatise Concerning Religious Affections* (1746), his final attempt at analyzing his observations during the 'Great Awakening' (the

Northampton 'revival'); it is shown almost equally in the much anthologized and famous but not easily understood "Personal Narrative" written, though not published save posthumously, in 1739, during the 'Great Awakening.'

The "Personal Narrative" appears uncompleted and was certainly not intended for publication. Most of it deals with his religious life up to twenty years before; but in the last pages there are references to "this town" of Northampton and the dates 1737 and 1739. Chronology and structure are difficult. Sometimes called "Narrative of His Conversion," the narrative—if it can be called that—undoubtedly was written by Edwards for his own instruction.

The English Puritans—many of whom migrated to New England—knew the experience called 'conversion': it was, in a sense, the outward sign of their Divine 'election.' It did not mean, commonly, that they had led lives of open sinfulness before; it meant a deepened sense, often preceded by torment and struggle, of man's natural depravity and of God's grace, a *turning* from all satisfaction in humanist virtues to the aspiration for true holiness.

The normal thing was to think that 'conversion' occurred, dramatically, but once. But, for some men (John Wesley and Edwards included) this classic pattern seem not to fit; and Edwards has, in effect, to deal with a series of *conversions*, successive deepenings both of the sense of sin and of the sense of grace. He was always, says he, concerned, from childhood, with his soul, but he had two "remarkable *seasons of awakening*" before he reached "that new *sense* of things" which was his last conversion.

The first occurred before he went to Yale, during a

'revival' within his clerical father's congregation. It seemed to Edwards later that this "first conversion" was —though he does not use the word—'Pharisaical.' Its pleasure—"self-righteous pleasure"—was in the abundance of "religious duties"—talking with other boys about religion, praying "five times a day in secret," feeling emotionally about God. This religious emotionalism or sentimentality, this "delight . . . in religion," seemed to Edwards later what men often mistake for "grace."

His second pseudo-conversion was almost opposite in character: now he practiced "many religious duties" but without any pleasure. "My concern now wrought more by inward *struggles* and *conflicts* and self-reflections." Yet this second 'conversion' was false—a "miserable seeking," prompted, apparently, by terror: belief in the truth of God's sovereignty but inability to see in it anything except a "horrible doctrine" which, nonetheless, being factually true, one had, out of self-interest, to act upon.

So there is a pseudo-conversion of self-righteous love and another of terror at what, intellectually, one makes out to be the grim reality of God's conduct of the world.

Edwards' third, and real, conversion (undated) appears to be the shift from emotional pleasure and intellectual acceptance to a more or less permanent state of accepting affectionally (as well as intellectually) the sovereignty of God and of having a *new and spiritual* sense of the combined Power and Love of God. About his new experience, he talked with his father; and then walking in his father's pasture for contemplation, there came into his mind "so sweet a sense of the glorious *majesty* and *grace* of God that I know not how to express. I seemed to see them together in a sweet conjunction, *majesty* and *meekness* joined together; it was a sweet and gentle and holy majesty, and also a majestic meekness, an awful sweetness, a high and great and holy gentleness." After his conversion, Edwards' religious experience seems to have three dominant notes: one is the *sweetness* (a word which, though he is conscious of its being an analogical term, he repeats over and over) of God. ["There is a difference between having a rational judgment that honey is sweet and having a sense of its sweetness. A man may have the former that knows not how honey tastes, but a man cannot have the latter unless he has an idea of the taste of honey in his mind."] The second 'note' is the desire to lose his finite self: he desires to be "emptied of myself and swallowed up in Christ," "an ardency of soul to be—what I know not otherwise how to express—*emptied* and *annihilated*, to lie in the dust and to be full of Christ alone . . ." If this seems 'pantheistic' or 'mystical,' Edwards knows the difficulty of adequate language. "Emptied" implies the figure of a vessel, a receptacle: the receptacle may structurally remain, but let it become a chalice filled with the not-self, God.

And, third, as Edwards grows spiritually aware, he becomes more cognizant of his own sin. The saint—it is a kind of axiom—is more sensitively conscious of his own sin than the sinner or the recently 'converted' sinner.

The expressions of this third 'note' are expressly dated as of Edwards' years after he became minister of Northampton. "I have had a vastly greater sense of my own wickedness and the badness of my heart *than ever I had before my conversion.*" "I have a much greater sense of my universal, exceeding dependence on God's grace and strength *and mere good pleasure*, of late, than I used formerly to have, and have experienced more of an *ab-*

horrence of my own righteousness. . . . And yet I am greatly afflicted with a proud and self-righteous spirit—much more *sensibly* than I used to be formerly."

The "Narrative" ends with a contrast between the "delight" which followed his first conversion and his present state. The last dated entry (1739) shows, in no morbid way, his 'Dark Night of the Soul'—his sense of what the Catholic ascetic and mystical writers whom, I think, he had never read would have approved: in the context, the very word *duty*, so dangerous to latter-day Protestants, takes a right, a spiritually healthy, place: "I had such a sense: how *sweet* and *blessed* a thing it was to walk in the way of *duty*." One feels that in this sentence, as in the early sentences about predestination, which Edwards "from childhood up" used to find "a horrible doctrine" until, upon his real conversion he, "very often," found it a doctrine exceeding pleasant, bright, and sweet"—one feels, I say, that the co-presence of "sweet" and "duty" is, rhetorically, an oxymoron. But more: The union of the two that 'duty' should be 'sweet' represents Edwards' ideal. "Duty" implies struggle and conflict; "sweetness," the transcendence: the "swallowing up" of the ethical dualism by the religious monism. The 'end of true virtue' is to love to do what one knows one ought to do.

Edwards was long in existentially achieving what, at times, he could see. As he admitted, he was "greatly afflicted with a proud and self-righteous spirit." He could humble himself before God; but among the men he knew—whether in Northampton or Boston—he never found his intellectual superior or, indeed, equal, and pride of intellect was likely his chief sin; and pride of intellect translated itself into other kinds of sin. He did not welcome criticism of the minister by the congregation; and, for all his deep faith in true religion as a matter of 'true religious affection,' not of academic education, he could not but be troubled by the emergence, during and after the Great Awakening, of uneducated laymen who, because they were, or believed themselves to be, 'converted,' denounced the academically educated parish clergy as incompetent to preach the Gospel and took this task upon themselves.

It can scarcely be doubted, too, that Edwards was conscious, before his painful dismissal from his parish, of hypocrisy in some degree—how much hypocrisy and still more how much consciousness of it, it is difficult to say. His feelings toward his grandfather, 'Pope Stoddard,' as whose junior colleague he was introduced into the pulpit of Northampton, must always have been mixed, but I suppose his final decision (sharpened by his study of revivals and 'conversion') must gradually have brought him to the decision which settled his fate: that of abolishing the 'Pope's' practice—to which the Mathers and Edward Taylor strongly objected—of taking all men not *visible sinners* into the church and giving them the Lord's Supper not as a token that they were 'converted' but as an aid, a propaedeutic, to the same.

The final Edwardsean position—for himself as well as for others—is a rigorism entirely opposite both to Stoddard's inclination to take a commonsense view of church membership (since we can't be sure who the invisible saints are, we might as well include any men who are not visibly sinners) and to Catholic humanism, which finds human affections and the sacraments a proper mode of leading men up the ladder to "disinterested benevolence" and God.

And so indeed Edwards ends, in his *Nature of True Virtue*, posthumously published. Edwards had read attentively "the most considerable of late writers on morality" (his phrase)—including the Cambridge Platonist Ralph Cudworth, Shaftesbury, Hutcheson, Hume. From Shaftesbury and Hutcheson comes the notion that there is a "moral sense . . . natural to all mankind [which] consists in a natural relish of the beauty of virtue." From such a doctrine, Edwards 'naturally' dissents. But the interesting chapter for my present purpose is that called "Of Natural Conscience and the Moral Sense."

Though far from infallible in either its *judgments* or its *insight*, conscience is, nonetheless, *formally* or *structurally* the voice of God within me. *Conscientia semper sequenda:* conscience is always to be obeyed. But I understand Bishop Wilson to be referring to *conscience* in its aspect of *guide* when he writes: "First, never go against the best light you have; secondly, take care that your light be not darkness." And St. Paul, followed by the early Greek Fathers, thinks of men as having an innate power of judging right, a Law universally written on the hearts of men, Gentile as well as Jew (Romans 2: 14–15).

None of these would Edwards, I suppose, deny; but, in his 'ultrasupernaturalism,' to use Msgr. Knox's useful word, he wishes to give all such operations—the "Moral Sense," to which Shaftesbury and Hutcheson appealed, and the 'conscience' as ordinarily conceived—the name of 'secondary virtue.' Classical theology, from St. Thomas Aquinas to Bishop Butler, has conceived of there being such a thing as 'Natural Religion' (provable by unaided human reason) and such another thing as 'Revealed Religion' (embracing doctrines like the Trinity and the Incarnation) not to be arrived at by reason even though, when revealed, found not contrary to reason.

Edwards uses 'natural' in such a sense when he writes "Of *Natural Conscience*, and the Moral Sense." What other kind of conscience is there, we ask? Edwards never precisely names it, but it is clear that this other kind is a supernatural conscience, the gift of Grace to the Elect.

His analysis of 'natural conscience' is a keen and (so far as it goes) persuasive tracing of it to what might be called a refined self-love: that is, there is "a disposition in man to be uneasy in a consciousness of being inconsistent with himself and, as it were, against himself in his own actions." Though Edwards does not cite the partial parallel, men are, in their vanity, uncomfortable and embarrassed if found inconsistent in their written or spoken thinking. But we may fairly judge men of a higher sort are "uneasy" and uncomfortable when, in the privacy of their studies or in the act of writing, made conscious of intellectual incoherence. Quite apart from the loftier motives, they would like, for their own *peace of mind*, to resolve the arguments which contend with one another in their minds.

Edwards now extends uneasiness at moral inconsistency (such as may spring from self-love) to a man's uneasiness "in the consciousness of doing that to them which he should be angry with them for doing to him, if they were in his case, and he in theirs." The 'Golden Rule,' it appears, is an injunction of 'natural conscience': an empathic consciousness of how much I should resent being treated as I might another. Edwards refrains from saying—perhaps doesn't even think—what comes to a twentieth-century mind: that I may refrain from mistreating others in order that I shan't have to fear their having 'legitimate' reason, should they acquire the power—have the opportunity—to mistreat me.

Though this may be true, probably no man would think of calling such precautionary action the work of his 'conscience.' Edwards seems clearly to be thinking of Shaftesbury, Hutcheson, and Bishop Butler, who view *benevolence* as the enlightened development of *self-love*. When men have acted towards others as they would think they should be acted towards, "then they have what is called *peace of conscience*. . . . And there is also an *approbation of conscience*. . . ." Primary in this approbation is "a sense of desert and approbation of that general agreement there is in manner and measure in justice." We are glad—perhaps even in an aesthetic way—to see what is our conception of *justice* being done—the righteous rewarded, the criminal punished—each with the right size of fine and the right length of jail sentence. It accords with a 'natural' pleasure in *order* to see people "get what is coming to them," or "get their just deserts."

But, to conclude Edwards' refutation, some men, "through the strength of vice in their hearts, will go on in sin *against clearer light and stronger convictions of conscience* than others. If conscience, *approving duty and disapproving sin*, were the same thing as the exercise of a virtuous principle of the heart *in loving duty* and *hating sin*, then *remorse of conscience* will *be the same thing as repentance*. . . ." But it patently is not.

'Natural' conscience *approves* of duty, recognizes justice and desert. These, however, are intellectual apprehensions—"judgments," but intellectual judgments. It is, doubtless, a good thing to *approve* duty; but 'true virtue,' which is for Edwards, it seems, religious virtue, or *holiness*, is not *approving* of duty but *loving* it: not disapproving of sin but *hating it*. This is a matter not of intellectual judgment but of the affections—of what twentieth-century Americans might call "the attitude" or the "total orientation."

So here, then, we have reached the chasm which separates ordinary virtue—what most people take to be virtue—"neighborliness," "sense of civic responsibility," and the like—from *supernatural* virtue, or *saintliness* (these are not Edwards' terms but mine). This "true virtue" is "loving or hating" actions from a sense of the primary *beauty* of true virtue—not for the self-approbation it will give one nor for any variety of utilitarian consequence, however refined: one loves beauty because it is beautiful. True virtue, "a divine principle," is "an agreement or union of heart to the great system [the universe] and to God the head of it, who is all and all in it. . . ."

How can a man *love duty?* Surely it is enough to ask him to make out what it is (not always easy) and then, however unwillingly, to do it. Isn't it asking the superhuman to ask me to *love it?* In the sense in which Edwards uses the term and in his context, it is clearly intended to be just that. Only the *converted* (who, viewed from God's side, are the *elect*)are capable of *loving* the *ought*. Edwards is not constructing a democratic ethics. Nor, of course, is he undertaking to say that he himself has achieved 'true virtue.' He is coolly content to define, as exactly as his language will permit, the 'highest grade' of goodness—that grade by reference to which all lower grades will be graphed or scaled.

HENRY DAVID THOREAU
(1817–62)

A Week on the Concord and Merrimack Rivers, published in 1849, purports to record an actual journey Thoreau made with his brother John in 1839; the actual journey is only a convenient, not too fussy, narrative device—as, one might well say, the building of a hut and planting of a garden are in *Walden* (1854), the only other book this man of many trades and pursuits published in his lifetime.[1]

Each day has its own entry, compounded of things seen, historical anecdotes of villages passed, poems (quoted or by Thoreau himself); but the six days of labor supply of themselves no symbolic hint. Sunday was an exception. What better day on which to attack what, in Concord and the rest of holy New England, passed for religion?

After some brief remarks about the rival claims of other religions ("the liberal deities of Greece" and "my Buddha"), and after some commendations of the ethnic Scriptures (of the Hindus, the Chinese, and the Persians), he offers a testimonial to the Christian Scriptures: "The New Testament is an invaluable book, though I confess to having been slightly prejudiced against it in my very early days by the church and the Sabbath school. . . ."

But all these levities and graceful acknowledgments are but preparation for some shrewd and hard-hitting attacks on Christian ignorance of what the New Testament means and, quite as earnestly, an attack on the anthropocentricity of the New Testament, an attack on 'goodness,' an attack on the New England *conscience.*

The New Testament would shock meeting-going Yankees if they really listened to it, and they are hypocrites that they don't. But then the New Testament itself "treats of man and man's so-called spiritual affairs too exclusively and is too constantly moral and personal to alone content me, who am not interested solely in man's religious or moral nature, or in man even."

As for conscience, it "really does not, and ought not to, monopolize the whole of our lives, any more than the heart or the head. It is as liable to disease as any other part." And here, or two sentences hereafter, Thoreau breaks out into a witty poem which one might call "The Sick Conscience and the Healthy" [2]:

> Conscience is instinct bred in the house,
> Feeling and Thinking propagate the sin
> By an unnatural breeding in and in.
> I say, Turn it out of doors,
> Into the moors.
> I love a life whose plot is simple,

And does not thicken with every pimple;
A soul so sound no sickly conscience binds it,
That makes the universe no worse than 't finds it.
I love an earnest soul,
Whose mighty joy and sorrow
Are not drowned in a bowl,
And brought to life to-morrow;
That lives one tragedy,
And not seventy;
A conscience worth keeping,
Laughing not weeping;
A conscience wise and steady,
And forever ready;
Not changing with events,
Dealing in compliments;
A conscience exercised about
Large things, where one *may* doubt,
I love a soul not all of wood,
Predestinated to be good,
But true to the backbone
Unto itself alone,
And false to none;
Born to its own affairs,
Its own joys and own cares;
By whom the work which God begun
Is finished, and not undone;
Taken up where he left off,
Whether to worship or to scoff;
If not good, why then evil,
If not good god, good devil.
Goodness!—you hypocrite, come out of that,
Live your life, do your work, then take your hat.
I have no patience towards
Such conscientious cowards.
Give me simple laboring folk,
Who love their work,
Whose virtue is a song
To cheer God along.

In close juxtaposition with his attack on the fussily scrupulous conscience comes his terse, shrewd observation on the 'vulgar' notion of goodness. "Men have," he says, "a singular desire to be *good* without being *good for anything*. . . ," on the assumption, Thoreau seems to imply, that such vague goodness will win them postmortem Heaven.

Such a conception of goodness makes virtue seem largely negative and, perhaps worse, something unattached to our 'weekday' life. But virtue isn't negative and nebulous: it grows out of our honest and conscientious and freely willed performance of our work, our vocation.[3]

If I am a professor, my duty—and what centrally matters, morally, even—is to prepare my lectures and correct my students' essays and examinations and keep my office hours. And so with the contractor, the engineer, the cobbler, the farmer, the surveyor: the central morality for him is to do his work honestly, not skimping or scanting in the necessary materials and time. The 'outer' is my honest performance of my vocation; the 'inner'—what corresponds, perhaps, to that subjective of *intentions* and *motives* which in philosophy from Kant to Kierkegaard has been made the *all* of ethics—is to be thought of as *willing* my vocation, seeing it not as the not-me which economic pressure or the like has forced upon me but as the *me* carried from 'the heart' or 'the mind' into act, a fulfillment of the *me* far better than the desire to be 'good' or vague aspirations to be idealistic. The morality of work is consciously *willing* the duties of the profession in which (for whatever biographical circumstances) I find myself engaged.

Thoreau certainly believed in this morality of work. Like Emerson, his first great teacher, he thinks of vocation less fixedly though assuredly not less rigorously. For the two great Concordians, profession and vocation, though they may overlap, are not the same. Emerson found himself, upon honest scrutiny, in the wrong profession; and the central problem of his life was certainly to discover his true vocation—that is, that to which his convictions and his talents *called* him. Eventually, he found both profession (or professions) and vocation: professions, traveling lecturer and author; vocation, to be, as Matthew Arnold said, "the friend of those who would live in the spirit" or as Emerson himself said to Elizabeth Peabody, "My special parish is young men inquiring their way of life." [4]

Thoreau's 'case' is parallel but more striking. He, too, had to 'support' himself; and he began by teaching school, tutoring, making lead pencils (a modest industry begun by his father). He even did a little lecturing for lyceums. But I suppose that the 'profession' at which he arrived and at which he persisted was that of surveyor. Says Emerson, in his memorial address: "A natural skill for mensuration, growing out of his mathematical knowledge and his habit of ascertaining the measures and distances of objects which interested him—the size of trees, the depth and extent of ponds and rivers, the height of mountains and the air-line distance of his favorite summits,—this . . . made him *drift* into the profession of land surveyor."

"Drift" gives, perhaps, a misleading turn; I don't know that Thoreau *drifted* into surveying any more than Emerson did into lecturing. The point in both instances was to experiment till you found a 'profession,' a way of earning a livelihood—which one could manage conscientiously to perform—but which was compatible with—perhaps was a kind of outward practical form of —one's vocation.

Both Emerson and Thoreau had what I am tempted to call the New England moral sense of thinking it shameful to be financially 'beholden' to any one. It is questionable to me whether self-support, even on the part of men, is so universally a moral obligation as they viewed it. An artist who works seriously at his art, supported as was E. A. Robinson for some years, seems to me not immoral. And so with a stimulating companion supported economically by those whom he supports intellectually or spiritually.

But I know that—at least to an older New Englander—such arrangements were embarrassing and, to the recipient, somewhat shameful public testimonies of weakness. One would wish to earn his living in a fashion publicly acceptable in a world where everyone *works*—not only the banker or the farmer but the novelist who regularly and copiously, like Balzac and Dickens, turns out novels which sell enough to support him and his family, or, even more especially novelists like Scott and Trollope, who write with *business-like* regularity of hours, never missing a day, and wherever they are—at home or traveling by train or plane—writers who are *regular* in their hours as a businessman or a Benedictine monk.

There are, I now see, intermediaries between profession or 'occupation' in its public, its external, sense and 'vocation,' that innermost calling, which, if one is so fortunate as to have one, one should probably not attempt to name. *Clergyman* and *surveyor* are occupations we can report to the census-taker; perhaps we can even report 'public lecturer.' But then we come to another level. Emerson and Thoreau *now* seem 'major American authors.' Was authorship, or writing, then, their profession? To his own generation, Emerson was an author and Thoreau (despite two unsuccessful books) was not. Both certainly wrote extraordinarily well—ultimately, in styles as different as the men. Yet neither seems, as Arnold felt and said of Emerson, what we ordinarily mean by a literary man, literary as Byron or Victor Hugo or Henry James or T. S. Eliot were literary men. One feels one has missed the point if one says their profession was that of author, and, in the case of Thoreau, one feels that the more sharply. Emerson says of him, "He declined to give up his large ambition of knowledge and action for *any narrow craft or profession*, aiming at a much more comprehensive calling [that is, vocation], the art of living well."

This "art," which is and is not quite equivalent to ethics, Thoreau learned in many ways and from many sources. It was learned from experiments like Walden, from his preferably solitary daily walks "cross-lots," from his nature studies, which hovered between loving the precision and accuracy of detailed observation of details—particular birds, flowers, weeds, and trees and, at the other pole, the desire to find the general laws, natural and spiritual, which lay behind or resided in the specificities—and from books, even—the older the better, the nearer to any theology—the scriptures of China and India.

Thoreau is a well-nigh consistently severe critic of what most Americans in his time—and yet more in ours—take for granted—the grand law of progress: the newest is the best, "modern living movements," "le dernier confort,"—most deliciously in his review of the strangely twentieth-century-sounding book by Etzler published in 1842, *The Paradise Within the Reach of All Men Without Labor, by Powers of Nature and Machinery*.[5]

Thoreau consistently denies cities and highways (now

called 'expressways') and civilization. When he left Concord, it was not to go to Europe but to Cape Cod or to Maine, where life was more primitive than in the town of Concord. In Concord he could find arrowheads, but in Maine he could find Indians, some of whom could still make them.

In all of this protestantism and primitivism Thoreau himself was willing (in his late essay "Walking") to admit to some exaggeration: "I would wish to speak a word for Nature, for *absolute freedom and wildness*..., to regard man as... a part and parcel of Nature, rather than a member of society. *I* wish to make an extreme statement, if so I may make an emphatic one, for there are enough champions of civilization: the minister, and the school-committee, and every one of you will take care of that."

In Transcendentalist days, there were two kinds of Apostles of the Newness. One kind was made up of those who would better the world by altering institutions, other people, some particular practice. Both Lowell and Emerson have written delicious accounts of the Chardon Street Convention held in Boston by the 'Friends of *Universal* Reform.'[6] By 1830 the chief reform groups were the 'Temperance' movement and the Abolitionist movement. But, with the American love of committees and organization, "collective action" formed societies "promoting home and foreign missionary enterprise, distributing Bibles and religious tracts.... There were innumerable lesser societies to promote peace among nations, to reform prisons..., to stop the carrying of mails on the Sabbath, and the wearing of corsets."[7] There were the Grahamites, precursors of the 'nature food' shops and propagandists; there were vegetarians of the more or less strict variety. There was a whole series of Utopian socialist communities, of which Brook Farm and Alcott's Fruitlands were only the most famous.

Both Emerson and his 'disciple' Thoreau took no part in these forms of 'collective action.' [8] Emerson, in his gentle and sanguine way, was much beset by visits from such reformers, listened to them courteously, but firmly declined to 'join' either Brook Farm or Fruitlands. Thoreau and he represented the second class of reformers, those who said—and practiced—'reform begins at home.' Reform yourself; *set an example*—though this sounds in phrasing too pious for either of them.

Their attitude—and they were both sceptical and satirical of Reformers (see Thoreau's remarks in the first chapter of *Walden*)—came down to two positions: one was that though a particular reform urged was desirable, in order to act effectually in its behalf you would have to neglect all the *other things* which equally need reforming, and you might well end, like Hollingsworth, the advocate of prison reform in Hawthorne's *Blithedale Romance*, a patent monomaniac.

The other 'position' was that from which both Emerson and Thoreau took off: Individualism, reforming yourself after thinking for yourself; not being a *joiner* (pronounced in rural Massachusetts still, a 'jiner'). "Self-Reliance" is one manifesto of Individualism, perhaps the most exaggerated and, so to say, Thoreauvian, overstatement Emerson ever made. The social criticism in *Walden*, notably the opening tirade so ironically titled by a word all Yankees swear by, "Economy," is criticism of society from a yet more violent and certainly far more tactless individualist than Emerson.

In 1846 Thoreau was put in jail for refusing to pay a poll tax. Four years earlier Alcott had been jailed for refusing to pay a poll tax to a government which permitted slavery to exist.

But the end of the Thoreau imprisonment I find anticlimactic. The poll tax was paid for him next day by his hard-working relatives, and he was released.

It is hard for me to see the bravery and logic of this famous incident. If this was 'passive resistance' to some particular action or inaction of the state of which Thoreau disapproved, surely he should have stayed in jail and urged others to join him there in his protest. Why allow someone else—Emerson or his sister—to pay the tax? Out of deference to their individual right to pay? This seems individualism not only absurd but immoral. Dorothy Day and her "Catholic Workers" have served out their jail sentences when, on principle, they refused to obey New York's rules for air-raid or whatever.

In 1849 Thoreau published his now famous essay called "Civil Disobedience," confusing and difficult even to summarize, let alone defend or refute. Gandhi, the Reverend Martin Luther King, and Dorothy Day, all "passive resisters" of our century, appear to have made something more consistent out of Thoreau's essay than did Thoreau.

Thoreau is certainly a 'philosophical anarchist.'[9] As he clearly says, "That government is best which governs not at all"; but he is willing, for the time being, to accept a more or less Jeffersonian position of "that government is best which governs least." There were in his time, apparently, people who called themselves "no-government men"; he, however, disclaims that 'philosophical anarchy' can be demanded at once. What can at once be demanded is "a better government."

He turns then to challenging the democratic principle of 'majority rule.' That seems to him passable if the majority is to decide only on the *expedient*, not more. "Can there not be a government in which majorities do not virtually decide right and wrong, but *conscience?* . . . [If not,] why has every man a conscience then?"

Thoreau seems to think quite self-evident the distinction between the *expedient* and the *moral*. But is it? And can one man's conscience be deemed so infallible that it can judge that it is immoral to choose the lesser of two evils—as one often has to choose the greater, or higher, of two duties?

"It is not desirable to cultivate a respect for the *law* so much as for the right." Most men are willing to serve the State, the representative of current law, with their bodies. But a "very few, as heroes, martyrs, reformers in the great sense, of *men*, serve the State with their *consciences* also, and *so necessarily resist it for the most part*." The "for the most part" is not clear; perhaps Thoreau does not mean that *most* of the laws are wrong, but that reformers and martyrs "for the most part" object to and resist one or another of the laws. In any case "they are commonly treated by it [the State] as enemies."

Now we come to the distinction between *revolution* and *resistance*. Writing in 1849, Thoreau says "All men recognize the right of revolution." Doubtless all Americans think the Revolution of 1775 was justified; but of course that Revolution confiscated the property of those whose consciences thought it not justified, and most 'Loyalists' fled the land. Very few Americans then or now would, however, agree with Jefferson's calm dictum that there ought to be a revolution every twenty-five years. And Americans, who now lag socially behind the 'free nations of Europe,' did not, with few exceptions, approve of the French Revolution, and still fewer, in our own century, approve of the Russian Revolution or of the Chinese. The maxim that all men "recognize the right of revolution" is highly dubious if meant as more than of revolutions long ago and in English-speaking countries.

"Revolution" I take to mean a bloody and "violent overthrow of the [existing] government"—as distinct from the British 'bloodless revolution' of 1688 or the Roosevelt revolution. But if men feel in their conscience that the existing government is taking a wrong course of action, confounding morality with expediency, such men—or one such man—must resist (here I am attempting to rephrase Thoreau).

Though the word *conscience*, for understandable reasons, was offensive to Thoreau, surely no one was ever more rigorously conscientious than he—more consciously aware that nearly everything is finally a moral choice. I inserted "nearly," suddenly remembering Thoreau's intense feeling that "wildness" must be a necessary counterbalance to 'the moral,' but I have to hesitate, since Thoreau's "wildness" appears never to mean brutality or sensuality but rather a quality as stoic as primitivism and doubtless also an interest in the nonhuman world, animate and inanimate, an interest in the objective, the not-me. The defiant plea for 'wildness' is a plea for manly rigor and endurance and practical sense as elements in the human character which must not be so refined away, polished, or civilized that man cannot adapt and endure. And if this reading be right, Thoreau's "wildness" is conscientious—a part of his deliberate ethical thinking and his life-practice.

There are occasional passages in "Civil Disobedience" which certainly seem texts for the 'passive resistance' of a group. It is ambiguous whether or not Thoreau thought of himself as an Abolitionist, but it is highly doubtful that he called himself one, and he is not thinking of himself but a small and active group led by William Lloyd Garrison when he says: "I do not hesitate to say that those who call themselves abolitionists should at once effectually withdraw their support, both in person and property, from the government and *not wait till they constitute a majority of one* before they suffer the right to prevail through them. I think that it is enough if they have God on their side, without waiting for that *other* one."

It is in the concluding sentence of the paragraph just quoted that Thoreau seems to be expressing his ultimate position: "Any [one] more right than his neighbors constitutes a majority of one already."

At times he seems to take the now familiar attitude that he will not pay taxes because he disapproves of a use, or some of the uses, to which the tax money is given —as a pacifist might refuse to pay our income tax today because more than half of it goes to keeping up our military establishment, either making war or preparing to engage in it as aggressor or defender. But he is capable, in this same essay which has proved so refractory to exegesis, of saying: "It is for no particular item in the tax-bill that I refuse to pay it. I simply wish to refuse allegiance to the State, to withdraw [as he did, early in life, from the Church] and stand aloof from it effectually.... In fact, I quietly declare war with the State, after my fashion, *though I will still make what use and get what advantage of her I can*, as is usual in such cases."

The "plea for Captain John Brown," which (despite the protest of the Abolitionists) Thoreau insisted on announcing and giving in the Town Hall of Concord, is a much easier piece to follow. Thoreau had twice met Brown in Concord, once at Emerson's house, and had been impressed by him. In his address he admits to knowing little of Captain Brown, and some of the facts he cites are, as we now know, inaccurate.[10] But Thoreau's "plea" has, on the face of it, far less to do with Abolitionism in any of its aspects than with John Brown's being a man of heroic individualism who, convinced of possessing a right conscience, did not wait for committees, organizations, or a majority to back him.

Brown was a native of Connecticut, and Thoreau sees in him a living representative of the best traits of the seventeenth-century Puritans, who "were neither Democrats nor Republicans, but men of simple habits, straightforward, *prayerful* [this thrown in to please a Concord audience, one thinks]; not thinking much of rulers who did not fear God, nor making mean compromises, nor seeking after available candidates." And then if *Puritan* were not enough a signal-word, a trigger-word, to his Concord audience, Thoreau also claims him as "a transcendentalist above all, a man of ideas and principles."

Though Thoreau's Aunt Maria and his sister Helen had been members of an abolitionist society, Thoreau never was a 'member.' Of course he *disapproved* of the Southern enslavement of the Negroes, but he was certainly aware of the Negro slaves who used to be in New England and of the traders in slaves like the deacon in Newport—of the ire roused by the neo-Calvinist minister of the Second Church of Newport, Dr. Hopkins, when he took his considered moral stand against it.[11] The chief thing, however, is to comprehend, as one can from the *Journals* and *Walden*, that Southern Negro slavery was to him, for the most part, not something isolate but a species of the philosophical genus *slavery*, the opposite of the again philosophical (that is, Platonic or abstract) genus freedom.

In the opening chapter of *Walden,* addressed to those "said to *live* in New England" (heavy irony), Thoreau speaks of farmers who are "serfs of the soil." And a few paragraphs farther on, he grows more direct in his naming: "I sometimes wonder that we can be so frivolous, I may almost say, as to attend to the *gross* but *somewhat foreign* form of servitude called Negro Slavery, there are so many keen and subtle masters that enslave both north and south. It is hard to have a southern overseer; it is worse to have a northern one; but worst of all when you are the slave-driver of yourself."

Men are slave drivers of themselves: working to amass money long after they have need. They are slaves of their lusts and ambitions; slaves of fashion and conformity; they are slaves of their own consciousness, so concerned with analyzing themselves that they can never transcend the solipsistic (not to mention the anthropomorphic) and survey with disinterested interest the birds, the flowers, the water, the clouds.

Thoreau died in 1862. There is not the least evidence that he did so with any but a *clear* (or as it is sometimes called, a *good*) conscience. In his last days and nights of pain he refused opiates, preferring—like the monks of the *Tibetan Book of the Dead*—to be clearly conscious to the end.

The *apothegmata morientum* of a great man have, for some, a special significance: Lord Chesterfield's "Show the gentleman a chair"; Goethe's "Light, more light." Thoreau's last whispered words were "Moose" and "Indians"; but his last articulated words—his last conscious words—are perhaps even more signal. On his deathbed an Abolitionist asked him about his belief in a future life, to which he replied, "One world at a time," and a theologically orthodox member of his family asked him if he had made his peace with God, to which he replied that he was not aware of ever having quarreled with him.

The 'lessons' to be drawn from Thoreau are difficult, indeed, to state. All my life, young Americans have, almost without exception, exalted Thoreau above Emerson. This is partly, doubtless, by way of reaction against the reverse estimate in the two friends' lifetime. But not entirely. I see Emerson as centrally poised midway between Thoreau and the Reformers (Ripley, Margaret Fuller, and the rest)—poised in a delicate and difficult equilibrium. The Reformers acted to change society, as socialists and communists have done in our time. As for Thoreau, the stock comment would be that he practiced what Emerson preached.

But try to ask what the effect of Thoreau has been. If one literally followed his example, one would have to remain a bachelor; otherwise conscience might make one feel responsible for the needs and education of a family. Diffuse Thoreau's 'lesson'—as the life of Christ or Christianity has been diffused—and it becomes something very vague: "plain living and high thinking," perhaps, or "we are all getting too materialistic these affluent days—too fond of *comfort* and *relaxation*, too much given to conformity, to the views of our neighbors." We read Thoreau and feel the better for hearing his 'idealistic' lesson, but are little less affected than Thoreau's Yankee neighbors were by reading the Bible or hearing it read to them in church. There is nothing in Thoreau, any more than in the Sermon on the Mount, which we—in our *condition in life*—can put into practice.

It seems to me that Emerson really achieved something more difficult and useful—what is called, I think, "living in the world but not being of it," or, more accurately, feeling always the need for some balance between the *prudential* and the *spiritual.* I still, after reconsideration, find something rigid and narrow about Thoreau's doctrines and an exaggeration in his style and tone which are absent from Emerson, who (like Cardinal Newman) can state an opponent's view (the atheist's in Newman's case, the conservative in Emerson's) with such calm and fairness that the opponent could not, himself, better the statement.

WILLIAM LLOYD GARRISON
(1805–79)

In 1830 William Lloyd Garrison, a native of Newburyport, served a seven months' sentence in the jail of Baltimore. His sons, in their *four*-volume life of their father, remark: "No man ever went to prison with a lighter heart or *cleaner conscience* than Garrison; and his slumbers, the first night, were as sweet and peaceful as if he had been in his old home by the Merrimac." The cause of his imprisonment: his having attacked, in a fashion adjudged libelous, a fellow-native of Newburyport engaged in the slave-trade, transporting Africans to New Orleans. The judgment and the imprisonment were in Baltimore, because from Baltimore was published, by a Quaker named Lundy and by Garrison (converted to Abolitionism by the Quaker), a weekly called *The Genius of Universal Emancipation.* It is characteristic of

Garrison that his libelous paragraphs were not directed at the South. The trade ship "Francis" belonged to a fellow townsman. "So much for New England principle!" And a week later "I merely wish to illustrate New England humanity and morality."

That latter-day saint John Jay Chapman (whose remarkable grandmother, Mrs. Maria Weston Chapman, was Garrison's female cohort) published in 1913 a book on Garrison full of fire and insights but difficult to follow, since the grandmother, still alive in the 1880's, brought him up with an intimate knowledge of the intricacies of the Abolitionist movement—which turns out to be as intricate as the history of New England theology or the controversies, parties, and shades of Highness, Lowness and Broadness in the nineteenth-century Church of England. "Among the true, inner-seal Garrisonians the *wrong kind* of anti-slavery was always considered as anti-Christ...." And so, though he shows that he really knew better, Chapman's *Garrison* assumes that his readers know all about the facts of Garrison's life and "the wrong kinds of anti-slavery" organizations and the "inner-seal" Garrisonians' assemblage of views on subjects other than the evil of Negro slavery.

But this assumed knowledge is worth knowing, and I shall try to give it briefly.

Garrison was not 'a Harvard man'—or indeed an educated man in any rigorous sense of the word. What he had learned was—like Franklin's and Whitman's learning—from newspapers: he was a printer and a copious reader, clipper from newspapers. In early life, he was a pious Baptist, and—as Matthew Arnold says of the English nonconformists—"he knew his Bible." He did indeed, and long after he shook the dust of the 'churches' off his feet and rejected any creeds he continued a constant reader of the King James Bible and a constant and remarkably apt quoter from it. The Hebrew Prophets were perhaps his particular favorites—quite naturally, for they, too, were reformers and the denouncers of wickedness in high places, ecclesiastical and political.

Out of jail, Garrison began to publish—and continued to publish for thirty-five years—the *Liberator*. It was issued from Boston, where Garrison narrowly escaped being killed by an angry mob, or at least being tarred and feathered. That pre-Civil War Boston was Abolitionist—the view I learned at school—is a legend. The cotton manufacturers of Massachusetts—and in consequence the business interests of Boston—were necessarily dependent on the Southern cotton planters and their slave workers. And Garrison and his earliest allies were not gentlefolk. When there gradually arose a group of aristocratic converts to the cause—men like Wendell Phillips and Charles Sumner—they were ostracized by Beacon Street as well as fought by State Street.

As for the Garrisonian brand of Abolitionism, Garrison (like his Quaker teacher, Lundy) was a pacifist. He was from the start opposed to the solution of shipping the Negroes back to Africa, the scheme of the one really respectable Abolitionist group, the Colonization Society, which was founded in 1816; and he published in 1832 a thick, closely reasoned pamphlet denouncing this solution as sham reform. At first willing to admit of gradual emancipation, by the time he published his inaugural editorial in the *Liberator*, he made "a full and unequivocal recantation" of "the popular but pernicious doctrine of *gradual* abolition." Then he ran into the fact (attested by the Missouri Compromise and the Fugitive Slave Law) that slavery is guaranteed by the American Constitution.

Garrison's answer was publicly to burn the Constitution and to appeal to the higher law of conscience. If slavery is constitutional, one shouldn't even wait for political alteration of the Constitution: one should, on purely moral grounds, defy it. After 1831 he attempted to win the support of the clergy of New England, with almost complete failure. The Episcopal bishop of Vermont published a *View of Slavery*, defending the institution from the New Testament; the chief orthodox Congregationalists, like Professor Moses Stuart of Andover, were equally obdurate. Whereupon, especially after 1835, the *Liberator* increased its attacks on the churches, attacks made into a violence combining the vitriol of journalism and the righteous indignation of the Old Testament prophets, of whom Jeremiah seems to have been Garrison's favorite. Garrison also attacked Sabbatarianism, the sanctity of the Puritan and Protestant Sunday, and eventually Biblicism—that is, the ascription of special extra-literary authority to the Bible. And he attacked the denial to women of full rights to speak in public and vote: women who had, indeed, proved almost his most valiant and resourceful defenders deserved their share in "Universal Emancipation."

In the third volume of *The Dial,* Emerson wrote briefly of a strange convention held in Boston in 1840 at the Chardon Street Chapel—a Convention of Friends of Universal Reform. The essay, written in Emerson's most brilliant narrative vein, has the same mixture of sympathy, satire, and detachment which appears in his "Historic Notes of Life and Letters in New England" (especially in the concluding section on Brook Farm) and in his character sketch of his step-grandfather, the Reverend Ezra Ripley. When, at last, I took in that Garrison was not *merely* an Abolitionist but an anti-

Sabbatarian and so on, I thought to myself Garrison must have attended that convention, and so he did. Three sessions of three days each were held by the Friends of Universal Reform (apparently not, either then or subsequently, an 'organization'): the first devoted to the Sabbath, the second to the Church, the third to the ministry. Such goings on seem out of keeping with the "American Way," so instinctively addicted to committees, programs, resolutions, and other organization mechanisms; but this convention lacked them all. The nine days were spent in exercise of the 'liberty of prophecying' or in "the elucidation of truth through free discussion" (Emerson's phrase). All in attendance had "their moment, if not their hour, wherein to chide, or pray, or preach, or protest." Those who attended showed "the pre-dominance of a certain plain, sylvan strength and earnestness," but "many of the most intellectual and cultivated persons attended its councils" —and here Emerson gives (without any epithets of identification) the remarkable list of Dr. Channing (the saintly minister of the Federal St. Church), Edward Taylor (Father Taylor of the Seaman's Bethel, the Methodist saint and untutored genius of sacred oratory), Bronson Alcott (Emerson's dear friend), Mr. Garrison, Mr. May (the Reverend Samuel May, brother-in-law of Alcott and Garrison's right-hand man, the saintly young Unitarian whose delicate insistence forced the famous Dr. Channing publicly to espouse Abolitionism is 1834 and to publish, two years later, a famous pamphlet on slavery which, though not pure Garrisonianism, was of immense service to the cause—the first published testimony by a man universally venerated in the South, North, and Great Britain), the Reverend Theodore Parker (leader of the *fourth* stage of Unitarianism, as

Channing and Emerson were of the second and third), Jones Very of Salem (mystic and poet and mystical poet, the best America has yet produced), and women also—including John Jay Chapman's Abolitionist grandmother.

"Universal Reform!" Garrison was much censured by his fellow Abolitionists for not limiting himself to the one ostensible cause for which the *Liberator* was founded —of course "Universal Reform" is the easiest thing to ridicule—the easiest thing not only for *practical* reformers and men of sense and judgment but even for philosophical idealists like Emerson (or even John Jay Chapman). Any practical man, even a practical reformer, will say, "One thing at a time. Yes, there are many evils and injustices which need to be corrected, but let's concentrate now on abolishing the evil which, in our judgment (or, more modestly, in terms of our temperament and its interests) most cries to Heaven for moral attention." On the other hand, Emerson and Thoreau, late and reluctant Abolitionists, for all their dislike of Reformers and even the very word, accepted the principle behind the grotesque phrase, 'Universal Reform,' and understood the philosophy of the matter much better than Garrison. The 'philosophy' is, of course, that everything is bound up with everything else: society needs something analogous to a *conversion experience*. And, second, the Concordians were deeply distrustful of mass conversion, or conversion by legislation or organization. Organizations are instruments of petrifaction; they rigidify and perpetuate half-truths or dead truths. "The letter [whether an ecclesiasticism, a secular organization, or a sacred book] killeth: the spirit giveth life." In any case, start at home: by converting yourself and then those geographically and psychically within reach of you.

I can well understand how John Jay Chapman, who wrote a book on Emerson and then one on Garrison (in the course of which Emerson always appears as an honorable foil) found in these two men his spiritual heroes and perhaps wasted his brilliant powers in trying to reconcile both in his thinking. It was a noble if Quixotic wish on his part to unite the active with the contemplative life. And, *from* such a view, also, Garrison is that *outer* of which Emerson is the *inner*.

They both belong, assuredly, to the Idea of the complete man; but a complete man, an unfallen Adam, would be "an island unto himself." In practice we have to accept some doctrine of degrees: that is, a given man is primarily (by the duty of his vocation, which is the duty of his nature) a thinker: but *primarily* does not exclude—nor, I think, exempt him from—exercizing, to a degree compatible with his primary duty, the obligations of a voter, a husband, a father, a member of the School Board, a 'good Samaritan.' Nonetheless, Jeremy Taylor ("Of Contentedness") says with wisdom: "If you covet learning, you must have leisure and a retired life; if to be a politician you must go abroad and get experience, and do all businesses, and have no leisure at all. . . . The dispersed excellences and blessings of many men, if given to one, would not make a handsome, but a monstrous fortune. *Use, therefore, that faculty which nature hath given thee, and thy education hath made actual, and thy calling hath made a duty*."

Garrison was not a monomaniac, devoted to the single idea of Abolitionism. Indeed, many Abolitionists censured him and his *Liberator* because, increasingly—

specifically, from its eighth volume on—he would not limit himself to one reform. Instead, he had to bring in nonresistance (or 'Passive Resistance'—a doctrine which he, characteristically, censured the Quakers for not carrying far enough), women's rights, total abstinence from alcoholic beverages, Perfectionism (akin to Wesleyan 'Holiness'—to which he was converted by the founder of the Oneida Community, John Humphrey Noyes): time would fail one to list all the doctrines Garrison gradually took unto himself. In an 'uneducated' kind of way, Garrison *was* a 'philosopher' for whom all of his causes—for all of which he could eloquently quote Scripture—were united. Chapman thinks, with some reason, that Garrison should have given up bothering with the organizational problems he was always encountering in keeping the Anti-Slavery cause 'pure' (that is, in accord with the ever-increasing number of beliefs and causes to which he had become converted) and just have devoted himself to running (and writing and editing) *The Liberator* as the personal organ of a prophetic spirit.

But this was, in terms of Garrison's personality—displayed to the point of tedium in his sons' biography of him—impossible. Like John Wesley and other leaders one could name, Garrison couldn't delegate power and couldn't, I think, have managed without balancing his doctrinal enthusiasms with the intense concern over every practical strategy of his organizational problems with conventions, large and small, promoting some of his allies, dropping and excommunicating former allies, arguing against the clergy. His letters show with what minute attention he followed the doings of friend, former friend turned foe, and just plain foe. He had a vast memory for the detail of names and faces. In reading *The*

Liberator we are perpetually on the battlefield and must be eternally vigilant.

Wesley wrote, at eighty-five, of "my never having lost a night's sleep, sick or well, at land or at sea, since I was born," and again, of having had "so little pain in my life, and so little sorrow, or *anxious care*." Garrison's testimony is little different. These were men who trusted themselves—or God (the distinction is not always clear, since they saw themselves as agents of God, as regents for Him on earth). They had hundreds of decisions to make, doctrinal and practical. The closest idealist could ponder each of these and often, like Lot's wife, "look back." Was that decision wise? Shouldn't I reverse it? Were my motives pure and disinterested, or was there in them some admixture of vanity or pride or the desire for power?

These are the things which produce sleeplessness and which sap the energy for action. Like Wesley, Garrison acted, spoke, and wrote as seemed right to him at the moment; then gave *the thing done* no further thought.

His writings in *The Liberator* are so violent and vituperative, whatever their subject, that they make the sensitive reader tremble not only for himself, "a sinner," or—by empathy—for the contemporaries of Garrison's damned and named, their names often in capital letters, but for Garrison himself, who somehow ought to have had more charity for those who differed from him doctrinally and more doubt whether or no his indictments—which scarcely distinguish between major and minor sins, mistaken brothers and criminal offenders—were just.

Garrison, however, appears to have felt none of these things; and of his often masterly invective Chapman (in his memoir of his grandmother) writes: "Garrison was never rancorous, *at least he was never really rancorous.* His rancor was political and done for effect [for moral effect, not histrionic, of course]. He assumed a tone of malevolence for rhetorical reasons [to move his readers to action, not to gratify their literary sensibilities]." Garrison read the Bible; and he read the newspapers of his time, violent in the language which one political party used of another. His style is a combination of Jeremiah and Bennett's New York *Tribune*, with, of course—partly for 'histrionic' and 'rhetorical' purposes—some degree of Messianic identification. "Woe unto you, scribes and Pharisees!" But he could put his armor on and off; and the testimony of family and friends is to his *private* meekness, mildness, and sweetness. This was not duplicity. His violence, even though it might and did involve name-calling, was addressed to issues and principles, not persons.

With the end of the Civil War, Garrison retired, if one can use that phrase of a man whose activities were self-imposed, but he did not retire in the sense of one who thought the millennium had come. I have never forgotten Albert Mordell's bitter words about Whittier: that after the War, he retired to Amesbury, quite unmindful that though the bond-slaves of the South had been emancipated, there were in Lowell and Lawrence, not far from him, the 'wage-slaves'—frail girls working in Massachusetts cotton mills for ten or twelve hours a day.

Not so, however, with Garrison. Only a few months before his death, he published in the New York *Tribune* an attack on Senator Blaine, of Maine, who sought to restrict Chinese immigration to California. He quickly discerned, and exposed, the 'race heresy' in a masterful letter, of which the conclusion runs: "Blaine declares,

'We have this day to choose whether we will have for the Pacific Coast the *civilization of Christ* or the civilization of Confucius.' Has he forgotten that, long before the advent of Christ, it was from the lips of Confucius came that Golden Rule which we are taught in the Gospel to follow as the rule of life in all our dealings with our fellowmen and which, carried into practice, will insure peace, happiness, and prosperity not only to the dwellers of the Pacific Coast but to *all peoples on the face of the whole earth.*

"This is not a personal controversy with Mr. Blaine, but a plea for human brotherhood as against all *caste assumptions* and clannish distinctions. . . ." [1]

Garrison did not die till 1879, but his real work, that of putting the issue of antislavery on a moral basis, was done during the decade 1830–40. Thereafter, the crusade was pursued on *political* grounds, by the Free Soil Party, out of which came the so-called Republican or Union-preserving party of Lincoln: developments of which Garrison could not in principle approve but of which (inconsistently and with a 'human' shifting from method to end, the emancipation of the Negro) he unofficially approved and rejoiced in.

The 'moral basis': this was not repudiated by later Abolitionists. In 1850, when President Fillmore signed the Fugitive Slave Bill, its New England opponents such as the Reverend Theodore Parker, based their defiance of the law on the principle of appealing from statute law to "higher law"—what Parker called "the eternal law of God." This "higher law" was not the law of the Commonwealth of Massachusetts against that of Virginia: it was a 'law' of conscience, binding only upon individuals who perceived it and acted upon it. How can it be *proved* that it is higher? It can't, save by its convincing those who don't accept it that those who do so act from disinterested motives and that the particular statute law which they defy can, by logical extension, be seen to involve a yet more general moral law which men of enlightened integrity cannot reject. Whatever Garrison's inconsistencies, one is struck by the fact that, writing a friend about his plea for the admission of Chinese "coolies" into California, he saw it as another illustration of the "caste assumption" which led the Southerners to deny freedom to the Negro.

Eventually, the action of the few "freedom riders" in the twentieth century and the Quaker and other "conscientious objectors" to military service may lead to a change in statute law. But Garrisonians ask, can we wait for "eventually"? What we see clearly as a moral issue must be settled—for ourselves, at least—by what they called (in contrast to "gradualism") "immediatism."

Supposing it accepted as final moral authority, as most people accepted it in Garrison's time, the Bible (an ecclesiastically authorized anthology of books written by many writers over a long period) cannot be expected to give an unequivocal answer to nineteenth- and twentieth-century problems. The Southern and other clergy could certainly show that slavery was tolerated not only in Old Testament but New Testament times. St. Paul writes to Titus, "Tell slaves always to obey their masters and try to please them, not to oppose or steal from them.... Remind men to accept and obey the constituted authorities..." (Goodspeed's tr.). And the same saint's views about women speaking in meeting are well known. The appeal of the 'reformer' has always to be from the *letter* of the Bible to its *spirit*. Not for Newman and Roman Catholics only is there—what

Newman so brilliantly expounded—a "development of doctrine."

Was Garrison a late incarnation of the Puritan? All a matter of definition. Of the Puritan suffering in England under Anglican oppression he was; of the New England Puritan, with his 'covenant theology' and his theocracy, his own 'group idea' imposed on all, he assuredly was not. In doctrine and practice, Garrison is much closer to George Fox and the seventeenth-century Quakers (whether in England or the Colonies) and to the Hicksite Quakers of the nineteenth century, who broke away doctrinally and practically from a Philadelphia orthodoxy and ritual which had become as rigid as other *unrenewed* institutional religions had become.

I have, lastly, to remark that Garrison is a signal instance of the 'good conscience,' that kind of conscience which the Puritans before their exodus and the early Quakers had. Like them, he 'suffered' for conscience' sake; he did not suffer from his conscience. The *moral* of my book is, probably, to show—to allow pleonasm—the pathological character of the *sick* conscience which is proud of its *sickness*. But I don't conceive of its opposite as the *good* conscience, which places *evil outside* itself. The opposite of sickness is health; and the healthy conscience is honest and resilient enough not to have to be self-righteous, a character which, not without reason, Garrison's critics (the enemies of righteousness he would have called them) accused him of. A man in so many respects to be admired, Garrison should, I think, have had a moderate capacity for self-questioning and self-criticism.

NATHANIEL HAWTHORNE
(1804–64)

New England has produced philosophers and poets. It has been singularly deficient, even down to the present, in providing writers of narrative fiction which could be called art. Sylvester Judd, a Unitarian minister, wrote *Margaret* (1845), a novel of much interest to the linguist and the folklorist and the student of transcendentalism. Dr. Holmes wrote three 'medicated novels' (of which *Elsie Venner* (1861) is the first and best); but they were 'medicated': *Elsie* was written to disprove Original Sin and Predestination as theology and to transfer the phenomena which seemed to justify the theological doctrines of Calvinism to the secular province of the medical man. Mrs. Stowe's most famous novel, *Uncle Tom's Cabin,* was written to free the slaves. Fiction must, for New England, be didactic; otherwise, it is a waste of precious time and the substitution of illusion for the profitable alternatives of biography and history.

It was a daring thing of Hawthorne to do to begin, with the publication, in 1828, of *Fanshawe,* a life devoted to the *art* of fiction.

Hawthorne's prefaces and prologues always have their interest, as bespeaking (so far as an essential solitary could) his private views. In the prologue to *The Scarlet Letter,* he speaks honestly, I think, as he recalls his ancestor—the "grave, bearded, sable-cloaked and steeple-crowned progenitor—who came so early, *with his Bible and his sword,*" who was a "bitter persecutor" of the Quakers, and his son, who "made himself so conspicuous in the martyrdom of the witches." "No aim that I have ever cherished would they regard as laudable...." " 'What is he?' murmurs one gray shadow of my forefathers to the other. 'A writer of story-books! What kind of business in life,—what mode of glorifying God—or being serviceable to mankind in his day and generation—may that be? Why the degenerate fellow might as well have been a fiddler!' "

But he adds, "Let them scorn me as they will, strong traits of their nature have intertwined themselves with mine."

This is a fair statement, I think, of the ultimate question about Hawthorne. Was he a neo-Calvinist who "saw [and believed] the empirical truth behind the Calvinistic symbols," or was he an artist who liked his gloomy subjects for "their picturesqueness, their rich gloominess"? In his brilliant early book on Hawthorne, Henry James argues for the latter view; others, like Herbert Schneider, have argued the former.

Both, I think, are right, and their views are reconcilable. Hawthorne didn't suffer from his conscience or fuss about it, and this is why he can be placed rather with the describers of the New England conscience than with those whom it dominated. But that Hawthorne's sympathies and attitudes are, with whatever qualifications, on the side of the Puritans rather than on that of the Emersonian Transcendentalists is clear both in his fictions and in his private utterances.

As James himself says, "Man's conscience was his theme..."; and again, he "had ample cognizance of the Puritan conscience;... looking into his own soul, he found *it* there."

It was there—in many forms, some of which have to be conjectured, others of which Hawthorne himself states in those half-ironical ways which protected his natural reticence.

He was embarrassed to 'tell a story,' to construct a downright fiction. It is extraordinary how few of the "tales" in his three books of alleged short stories are really tales—how many of them are 'sketches,' half-essays and meditations like "Fancy's Show Box" and "The Haunted Mind," how many take refuge as scenes from New England history (like "The Maypole of Merry Mount" and "The Grey Champion") or as allegories and parables (like "The Wedding Knell" and "The Minister's Black Veil" or "The Procession of Life," "The Christmas Banquet," "The Intelligence Office," and "A Virtuoso's Collection").

It is there in his half-ironical Preface to *The House of the Seven Gables:* "Many writers lay very great stress upon some definite moral purpose at which they profess to aim their works. Not to be deficient in this particular, the author has provided himself with a moral.... [But] when romances really teach anything, or produce any effective operation, it is usually through a far more subtle process than the ostensible one. The author has considered it hardly worth his while, therefore, relentlessly to impale this story with its moral as with an iron rod,—or, rather, as by sticking a pin through a butterfly. . . ."

It is there in his *American Notebooks*, which partly stores up themes for possible tales, partly seems exercises in writing. Like Edwards on the Flying Spiders, he is, in them, a shrewd, hard recorder, passing no moral judgments, indeed, abnormally cool and distanced from anything save precise observation and equally precise denotation. Hawthorne was not, indeed, sentimental or 'idealistic.' In his own way he was as relentlessly objective as Edwards (disguised, as this sometimes is, by his nineteenth-century techniques).

As an artist, writing about conscience, he "worked up" his subject through reading New England town histories, the books of Increase and Cotton Mather, Bishop Jeremy Taylor on cases of conscience, the Newgate Calendar, The State Trials of England.[1]

But, as an artist, his main business was to assimilate, to meditate; and when it came to dealing with his theme —the Puritan conscience, the guilty conscience, the conviction of sin, Hawthorne had to think and feel it all out for himself—operating (like most artists) rather by instinct and intuition than by 'reading up' on theology and ethics. He was repelled by Reformers, like his sister-in-law, Elizabeth Peabody; he was unable to find anything save sweet vagueness in Emerson (about whom his wife rhapsodized). But when he looked into the seventeenth-century Puritans, though he didn't try to follow their argument, he could see that they were arguing and serious about things which—call them by other names if one would—one ought to be serious about.

There are sins which certainly seemed central to him

—and they are all 'deadly sins,' for they destroy their possessors. The first is pride, the "insulating" pride which isolates one from 'all those others' ("Lady Eleanor's Mantle," "The Man of Adamant," "Ethan Brand," "Egotism; or the Boston Serpent").

Pride is protean: assumes innumerable forms—so much so that the sensible Franklin, after trying for humility, gave up the effort to do more than achieve the appearance of it, concluding that "if I could conceive that I had completely overcome" pride, "I should probably be proud of my humility." We are proud of our learning, proud of ignorance; of our sensibility, of our insensibility; of our health, of our illness. . . .

But these are all forms of pride in the self. Can't we get *out* of *ourselves?* Perhaps, if we are willing to be cold and impersonal, to view other men as statistics, as data for our computer machine. But then, of course, we haven't got out of ourselves: we have merely denied the reality of other selves, and left ourself the only self—that is, God.

Then there is concealment: hypocrisy would be the obvious word, but is the name of something much cruder than concealment. Hypocrisy is concealment practiced on others; concealment, however, has many tints and shades of that subtler thing, self-deception.

Then there is the domination of one person by another. The reality of witchcraft lay in possessing this power; and Hawthorne (as one sees in *The House of the Seven Gables*) viewed nineteenth-century mesmerism as a manifestation of the same force under a different name.

And lastly there is total skepticism, which (from one point of view) is despair.

Unlike Melville, Hawthorne did not need any theological absolutism. He had a deep faith not bound to dogma or clericalism or Biblicism—a deep faith which was nearer to Calvinism than to any nineteenth-century view—which was skeptical of humanitarian reforms, skeptical of traditional aristocracy, skeptical of solutions to the enigma of life. His skepticisms were of neat and total solutions, of panaceas. His faith—almost wordless, certainly creedless—was in 'accepting the universe'—in humility, in loyalty to persons and principles, in love.[2]

But in putting these words, these abstract nouns down, I feel how false to Hawthorne they are. To name the highest is to profane it. So the positive in Hawthorne is chiefly expressed through narrative and symbol, and the failure at the end of his life is to have feelings which can't find their right symbols and symbolic images which can't find their correspondent feelings.

The word 'conscience' is not common in Hawthorne: the 'thing' is partly thought of as a rigorous integrity, partly split up into its component parts. But a few examples may be cited: "Nothing is more remarkable than the various deceptions by which guilt conceals itself from the perpetrator's conscience . . ." ("The Procession of Life"). Roderick made his bosom serpent "the type of each man's fatal error, or hoarded sin, or unjust conscience" ("Egotism").

Hawthorne's two tales of conscience which seem most memorable are "Young Goodman Brown" and "Roger Malvin's Burial."

The former is both bitter and ambiguous. After three months of marriage, the young husband pleads the necessity of a strange journey into the wilderness—one between sunset and sunrise. This strange errand is to have a taste of evil before settling down to conformity. After "this one night I'll cling to my wife's skirts and follow her to heaven"—with which "excellent resolve for the future, Goodman Brown felt himself justified in making more haste on his present evil purpose." He soon meets Satan, an older man with a serpent-like walking stick. And then come all the old pious folk of Salem, also journeying, but not for the first time, into the 'heathen wilderness.' When a pink ribbon, such as his wife Faith had worn when he left her, comes fluttering down, the young man gives up. "There is no good on earth; and sin is but a name." As the company grows, it is clear that it includes both supposedly pious and supposedly evil impious people alike.

I suppose this story to have several interpretations: one, that of Satan's own speech to the assembled company: "*Depending upon one another's hearts*, ye had still hoped that virtue were not all a dream. . . . [But] Evil is the nature of mankind." The world isn't divided neatly into the good and evil. And our faith must not depend on the supposed absolute goodness of others; it must not even depend upon faith in Faith. Hawthorne doesn't go on to say it must not depend on anything or anyone save God.

And the second: Young Goodman Brown, by his own act of going into the Forest three months after his marriage, has already shown his lack of faith in the humanly good but not absolutely good in Christian civilization —marriage, including his own, the church, men's best efforts. He would not have gone into the Forest unless he had already doubted.

This was a dream, of course, but the dream of a self-centered perfectionist: the thing closest to it in Hawthorne is the chapter in *The Scarlet Letter*, "The Minister in a Maze," narrating Dimmesdale's walk home from the heathen Forest in which, persuaded by Hester that he can escape his own duplicity, he feels every temptation to express all his deeply hidden doubts and to shock all those whose goodness relies upon his saintliness. Dimmesdale makes the moral escape, dying as soon as it is made, but Brown suffers the rest of his life from the despair which this vision of the world induces.

Reuben Bourne is another "sad and downcast man." In the eighteenth century, a little group of colonists gave battle to twice their number of Indians, and that in Indian territory. Few of the whites escaped.

Roger Malvin, past middle age, had so serious a wound that he doubted he could go on. His younger companion, Reuben, also seriously wounded, had the advantage of youth and was affianced to Malvin's daughter, Dorcas. A long dialectic follows: Shall Reuben leave Roger or stay with him, perhaps with death as the end for both? The interplay of motives behind what one says and the interplay of motives behind what one does are subtly represented: Hawthorne never excelled this descriptive analysis of how mixed all our motives are.

Reuben, "but half convinced that he was acting rightly"—even though Roger has done most of the urging—receives the parting injunction that when he is well he return to this rock—"not unlike a gigantic gravestone"—and bury the body, and Reuben promises.

The younger man is long retarded in reaching the frontiers; his wounds finally cause him to lie down beneath a tree to die. He is rescued by the first rescue party and nursed back to health by Dorcas. But he is, long, too tired to talk.

Then comes the second dialectic. Dorcas asks him about her father, and Reuben begins a long, vehement reply, "defending himself against an imaginary accusation." Before he is done, Dorcas, anticipating, breaks in,

"He died!" "Reuben felt it impossible to acknowledge that his selfish love of life had hurried him away before her father's fate was decided. He spoke not..." His silence gave consent.

Dorcas' question which follows, "You dug a grave for my poor father in the wilderness, Reuben?" is answered by a statement literally true but as surely deceptive, and meant to be, to her who listened. And when the youth is well enough to totter from his sick chamber, he "experienced from every tongue the miserable and humiliating torture of unmerited praise." In this mixture of literal truth and the at once comforting and tormenting knowledge that others will misinterpret it to the speaker's glory there is a clear prefigurement of Dimmesdale in his pulpit: his self-denunciations, his concealing revealings.

The marriage takes place, but the paragraph following the mention of the fact is one of brilliant and subtle analysis too long to quote beyond this: "... concealment had imparted to a justifiable act much of the secret effect of guilt: and Reuben, while reason told him that he had done right, experienced in no small degree the mental horrors which punish the perpetrator of undiscovered crime."

He becomes, like Young Goodman Brown, sad, downcast, and his "secret thoughts and *insulated* emotions" have gradually made him irritable. His irritability involves him in lawsuits. He is finally a ruined man, and the only hope for him and his wife and his fifteen-year old son Cyrus, the one person really dear to him, is to strike out into the forest, clear away enough timber for settlement, and start again. Cyrus bounds off to kill a deer for their food. In his absence, Reuben, an experienced marksman, thinks he hears an animal in the thicket. He fires, and presently finds that he has killed his son, who is lying on that same ledge of rock upon which Malvin had been left.

"Then Reuben's heart was stricken, and the tears gushed out like water from a rock. . . . His sin was expiated,—the curse was gone from him, and in the hour when he had shed blood dearer to him than his own, a prayer, the first for years, went up to heaven from the lips of Reuben Bourne."

This tale is mistakenly read, I think, if read too theologically—as the last paragraph seems to give some pretext for doing. Tears gush forth, and Bourne can pray again: both are natural expressions which years of concealment and living a lie have made impossible. But the whole texture of the story is composed of the 'shall I; shan't I,' the mixture of motives, the hesitations and equivocations which may beset a sensitive man even when he has committed no crime, no sin. The texture of the story is less ethical than psychological. It is a psychological study of conscience.[3]

But Hawthorne is ever aware of that psychological and ethical world which joins the sin committed and the sin thought, felt, envisaged, and he brilliantly presents it in "Fancy's Show Box," with its awful pictures, embodying "the ghosts of all the never perpetrated sins" that glide through the mind of an old man. Conscience is relentless in presenting these pictures, but conscience may be too relentless, and confound entirely the possibility with the act. Yet, even so, "Man must not disclaim his brotherhood, even with the guiltiest, since, though his hand be clean, his heart has surely been polluted by the flitting phantoms of iniquity. He must feel that, when he shall knock at the gate of heaven, no semblance of an unspotted life can entitle him to entrance there. Penitence must kneel, and Mercy come from the footstool of the throne, or that golden gate will never open!"

HENRY JAMES
(1843–1916)

James, not a New Englander by birth, was an attentive observer and analyst of its conscience.

His father was the highly critical friend and correspondent of Emerson; his younger brothers attended the school of Frank Sanborn at Concord. The family home settled down to be Ashburton Place, Boston. And the 'literary' Henry had the advantage of his father's friends and position: his first published story appeared in the *Atlantic Monthly*.

In three of his novels (and many of his shorter fictions like "Four Meetings" and "Europe") James employed himself in the close description and analysis of something at once alien and repellent but also, with civilized improvement, an ineradicable part of himself.

(1)

In that little masterpiece, *The Europeans* (1878), he gave an ironical-pastoral depiction of New England in the 1840's, the age of Channing Unitarianism as well as of Transcendentalism. The 'Europeans'—the morganatic wife of a German princeling and her brother Felix, both adventurers in their several ways— have a New England uncle, Mr. Wentworth, and we see the Wentworths through the expatriates' eyes and the expatriates through the eyes of the Wentworths.

The sister and brother, who make their American stay in a cottage put at their disposal by their uncle, are discussed by him and his daughters "with a great deal of earnestness and subtlety." In this discussion, pleasure, excitement, entertainment play no part. "The sudden irruption into the well-ordered consciousness of the Wentworths of an element not allowed for in its scheme of usual obligations required a readjustment of that sense of responsibility which constituted its principal furniture.... The arrival of Felix and his sister was a satisfaction, but it was singularly joyless and inelastic satisfaction. It was an extension of duty.... What seemed paramount in this abrupt enlargement of Mr. Wentworth's sympathies and those of his daughters was an extension of the field of possible mistakes; and the doctrine, as it may almost be called, of the oppressive gravity of mistakes [a doctrine which may be called the New England Unitarian equivalent of *sins*] was one of the most cherished traditions of the Wentworth family."

Reporting his introductory visit to his sister, Felix, the 'European,' meets her comment: "They must be Puritans to their fingertips; anything but gay." "No, they are not gay," he admits. "They are sober; they are even severe. They are even of a pensive cast; they take things hard . . . they have some melancholy memory or some *depressing expectation.* It's not the epicurean temperament. My uncle, Mr. Wentworth, is a tremendously high-toned old fellow; he looks as if he were undergoing martyrdom, not by fire, but by freezing."

When the sister, the Baroness Eugenia, comes to call with her brother, Mr. Wentworth looks "very rigid and grave" and "almost cadaverous"; but Felix's "light imagination had gained a glimpse of Mr. Wentworth's spiritual mechanism, and taught him that the old man, being *infinitely conscientious*, the special operating conscience within him announced itself by several of the indications of physical faintness." This is naturally a grave occasion for a man so infinitely conscientious: how to treat a lady "at once so distinguished and so unhappy," and also, presumably, as a Catholic and European, so refinedly corrupt.

The Wentworths' Baroness has chosen, as the most eligible candidate for her worldly hand, the most worldly of the Wentworths' circle, a man who has been in the China trade. But she blunders. First in this novel, James begins his explorations—always casuistical and not dogmatic—of the difference between falsehood and truth, and though Robert Acton has got beyond the delusive simplicity of 'Never tell a lie,' he has some empirical conception of kinds and grades of lying. The ultimate defeat of the Baroness is anticipated when, first meeting Acton's invalid mother, she does not lie with mere ritual politeness but, in reply to Mrs. Acton's "I have heard a great deal about you," overdoes her lie: "From your son, eh? . . . He has talked to me immensely of you. Oh, he talks of you as you would like . . . ; as such a son *must* talk of such a mother!" James adds that the Baroness "instantly felt that she had been observed to be fibbing. *She had struck a false note.*" The sentence, the pianistic metaphor I italicize, is the real point. She has underestimated the intelligence and taste of her hostess; her lie has been too exuberantly, too flamboyantly, a lie. *Conscience* has its taste, its sensibility.

(2)

In 1886 James published a masterly novel, *The Bostonians.* The novel was a public failure, both in England and America. The title was perhaps fair ground for local grievance, since James makes no effort to portray either the surviving world of pre-Civil War Boston intellectual society—either the world of Mr. and Mrs. James T. Fields (of Ticknor and Fields) or the world of 'cold roast beef' Boston, the world of the solid bankers and merchants like the Forbeses and the Lawrences and the Lowells.

James's brother William, professor at Harvard, protested that everyone in Boston recognized in Miss Birdseye the venerable Elizabeth Peabody, Hawthorne's sister-in-law, Alcott's assistant at the famously progressive Temple School, Dr. Channing's amanuensis (just to mention her under a few of her philanthropic appositives). Henry protested. But why? Miss Birdseye is probably the most living and lovable character of the novel—quaint, absurd, senile, but most living and lovable—the real exemplar of Garrison's Universal Reform. As the novel ostensibly turns on the Women's Rights Movement, Miss Birdseye is naturally presented as an advocate of that movement. But, in her dying days, her mind most reverts to the "great work of her life, her mission, repeated year after year, among the Southern blacks. She had gone among them . . . to teach them to read and write; she had carried them Bibles. . . ."

The male hero of the novel is a Southerner who has fought on the Southern side, whose family has been ruined by the War, who is a rank conservative in his political philosophy: in his private vision of reform, "the first principle of it was to reform the reformers." But Miss Birdseye is too batteredly benevolent a universal reformer to arouse his hostility—or James's either. Her face—as Ransom first saw it—"looked as if it had been soaked, blurred, and made vague by exposure to some slow dissolvent." Miss Birdseye has no more "conscience" in that latter-day sense than Emerson: there is no struggle between duty and inclination.

The pathological 'New England conscience' in the book is that of Olive Chancellor, a cultivated, tense, 'high-strung' advocate of women's rights who ill understands herself. In his *Notebooks*, James conceived of the novel as "a study of one of those friendships between women which are so common in New England." No doubt James (like Dickens and Dostoevski) understood 'relationships' which only much later were to be named. The particular "friendship" dealt with *in* this novel is largely one-sided: Miss Chancellor has managed to channel most of her grievances against life into suspicion of men—men, as one might say, 'throughout the ages'; and she seems less privately fond of Verena Tarrant than eager to rescue her from her natural liking of men and to educate her for the great Cause.

Her constant theme, which she endeavors to trace through history—her ikon for meditation—is "the image of the unhappiness of women": she does not recognize how much that is her own intense nature projected through a magnifying glass. She must, of necessity, consort with her fellow reformers; but almost without exception they are distasteful to her. The eminent orator of the cause, Mrs. Farrinder, who lives in Roxbury, does not get the social stratification of Boston, of Beacon Hill, aright; most of the others, like Verena's parents, the Tarrants, are simply vulgar. Contention is, to her, the sweetest of delights, yet its outcome is tears, headaches, a day or two in bed—the luxuries allowed her by her income. She rightly fears Verena's taste for young men and even marriage, but does not understand that she wants to keep Verena for herself. She extracts a promise from the girl not to marry, only to give up what she has extracted: realizing, theoretically, that one must not intimidate or cajole others even into virtue, yet "she wished to extract a certainty at the same time that she wished to deprecate a pledge."

Beneath all these self-deceptions lies the New Englandly pathological desire "to look out for duties, to appeal to her conscience for tasks . . ."; and finally, the secret and sacred desire "to be a martyr and die for something."

But, alas (as Verena once says to Olive, "You are my conscience"), the male and Southerner wins out; and Olive's martyrdom never passes the limits of the difficulty of living.

(3)

In 1895 a young friend's mention of Howells as in Paris, where he "had scarcely been . . . even in former days," and of Howells' injunction to the young friend, "Live all you can: it's a mistake not to . . . I haven't done so—and now I'm old. It's too late," starts in James's mind the theme of *The Ambassadors.* His long Notebook entry of 1895 and the 20,000 word Prospectus for the novel, sent about 1900 to Harpers and now available in the *Notebooks*, make clear the extent to which this novel was James's most serious, as well as final, dealing with the New England conscience.

The *Notebooks* entries are conceptual and explicit in a way James as an artist would never be—and is not—in his novel. His 'hero,' suggested by Howells, the convert to Boston, is a man "who hasn't 'lived,' hasn't at all in the sense of sensations, passions, impulses, pleasures.... He has never really enjoyed—he has lived only for Duty [capitalized] and *conscience—his conception of them;* ... lived for effort, for surrender, abstention, sacrifice." "He has married very young, and austerely. Happily enough, but charmlessly and, oh, so conscientiously: a wife replete with the New England conscience." Now long a widower, he has been taken under the financial and moral protection of a New England and wealthy widow, an imposing figure in her city—some place like Providence, Worcester, or Hartford. She is, says James, a reflection of Strether's pre-European initiation; as befits the American world, the woman is "of the strenuous pattern"—Strether of the passive. She is will without imagination—unlike "poor Strether," who, despite his conscientiousness, has "imagination," that is, can conceive of other ways of being right than in his own suffering way.

Both Mrs. Newsome and Strether have New England consciences, but their consciences are of different species. Strether is said, in *The Ambassadors,* to arrive in Paris weary, perhaps on the verge of breakdown; but the representation scarcely bears out the assertion: he is, rather, frustrate at the ineffectuality of his life's efforts and mildly puzzled that being good has not made him happy.

Mrs. Newsome has no qualms on that score. She knows that we were not put here on earth to be happy, and her worries are not puzzles about herself. She must expiate, by her philanthropy, the unscrupulous ways by which her late husband left her wealthy; she must save her son, who has been for a few years in Paris, studying art and love, and who is presumably detained from returning to the unscrupulous promotion of her late husband's business by a sordid sexual attachment; she also is a woman of what used to be called 'culture and refinement,' and hence unavoidably distressed by, as well as with familial piety attached to, her daughter, not so cultured and refined, and her daughter's husband, who is even less so.

As a woman of force, Mrs. Newsome is a kind of New England counterpart of Aunt Maud Lowder in *The Wings of the Dove;* but the difference between two types of Anglo-Saxons is rendered perfectly and—not at all strangely—in accord with Hawthorne's impressions of the two in *Our Old Home*. Mrs. Lowder is untroubled by conscience or nerves: she is Britannia seated on her moneybags and ruling the waves, while Mrs. Newsome is a beautiful specimen of one kind of late nineteenth-century American woman: when James says, in his characteristic way, that she is "a really remarkable woman," he does not mean to praise her but to delight in her being so remarkably pure a specimen of a type. She is "high, strenuous, nervous, 'intense' (oh, a type)—*full of ideals and activities*"—a delicious phrase. "She is many other things besides; invalidic, exalted, depressed, at once shrill and muffled, at once abounding and extremely narrow . . . she is a particularly intense and energetic invalid," ever active, by virtue of her "restless conscience"—one, of course, directed towards others—in charities, reforms, and good works.

Mrs. Newsome loves Strether, "poor fine melancholy, missing, striving Strether": all of James's later sensitively passive men are Strethers; but he is not reported in the *Notebooks* as doing more than admiring and esteeming her. Indeed, though James can never bring either himself or Strether to say so, they both almost certainly fear and somewhat dislike her, though James has the advantage over Strether of seeing her as comic as well as—what Strether comes to see her as—narrow and unimaginatively righteous. Talking of her to Maria Gostrey, "his eyes might have been fixing some particularly large iceberg in a cool blue northern sea." Maria rejoins, "There's nothing so magnificent—for making others feel you—as to have no imagination." With full confidence in truth, undeniable in the sense intended, James successfully makes Mrs. Newsome, the unimaginative, present in the novel only through the force she exerts on the imagination.

At the instigation of Mrs. Newsome, Strether sets out for Paris to rescue Chad from his un-New England ways. The manifest irony is that, finding Chad vastly—and for the reader, somewhat incredibly—improved over his earlier self, at least temporarily, and in Strether's eyes, Strether is forced to a conception of salvation opposite to that with which he came. To save Chad is not to take him back to Worcester, Mass., but to keep him from returning. In this he finally fails. Chad's somewhat incredible elegance is attributable to the influence upon him of a Catholic noblewoman who, by her code, cannot marry him. As the *Notebooks* make more explicit than the novel, there is much of the unscrupulous late Mr. Newsome in Chad, and at the end of the novel he is fascinatedly studying that peculiarly unsavory American art, the art of advertising, and about to become a successful businessman at Worcester.

But Chad's failure to be, only to seem, a man of imagination—the passive, borrowed, and temporary quality of his civilizing—is only incidental to James's book. Its real subject, as well as its point of view, is Strether. Its real theme is the inadequacy of the famous New England conscience. Strether—and apparently Mrs. Newsome—are not even Unitarians; but, as for conscience, each has been accustomed to accuse the other of being "morbid"—that is, over-beset by the sense of guilt and the sense of duty; and they both hold inflexibly to the conception that happiness is dangerous—if not indeed evil.

What occurs to Strether in his three or four months in Europe can be called either the development of conscience into consciousness—or the change from the view of conscience as identical with its early presuppositions and mandates to the view that conscience is educable.

James calls his novel *The Ambassadors* for the sake of the comic and the ironic, but it might more seriously have been called *The Instructors* or—had not he earlier used that title with delicate irony for a delicate and masterful *nouvelle*—"The Pupil." The novel is a novel of initiation, a *Bildungsroman.* Strether's instructors are Miss Gostrey, Chad, little Bilham, Mme de Vionnet.

The first named is the most explicit and pedagogic. She takes her disciple in hand from his arrival at Liverpool and relinquishes her commentaries only when she feels sure that he can "toddle alone," and she establishes immediately an intellectual intimacy which makes him feel disloyal to the betrothed Mrs. Newsome.

Miss Gostrey directly sets to work on Strether. Strolling with her through Chester, Strether feels delight in the picturesque, dim memories of his former visit at twenty-five, but also conscience. His observant mentor quickly comments, "You're doing something that you think not right." The dialogue on the sin of even pleasure goes on, with Strether's question, "Am I enjoying it as much as that?" and Maria's replying, adapting herself to a New Englander by reminding him that pleasure may be a duty, "You're not enjoying it, I think, so much as you ought," and Strether's presently saying, "Woollett [the name finally adopted for Worcester] isn't sure it ought to enjoy." His guide responds, "I wish you would let me show you how to enjoy."

But, thus committing himself, he confesses to fearing, and he further expands the plight of the man beset by duties: "I'm always considering something else, something else, I mean, than the thing of the moment." Rebuked, he says, he knows he shouldn't. "If only I could! But that's the deuce of it—that I never can."

Paris abounds in surprises for Strether. He attempts to do his manifest duty. He indites long letters to Mrs. Newsome, long ambassadorial reports on things seen and heard, and as regularly for a time receives long replies from Woollett. But the time comes when Woollett letters cease, and a cable demands the ambassador's immediate return. He defies it, only to learn that his post is to be occupied by newly appointed and more sturdy legates. They come; before they depart, Mrs. Newsome's daughter Sarah summons Strether that he may make his submission. As Mrs. Newsome is "essentially all moral pressure," so, through Sarah, she "reaches him by the lengthened arm of the spirit." Still he resists, and Sarah has to remonstrate against his attitude toward the relation between Chad and Mme de Vionnet—his acting as though there could be a doubt, as between Chad's loyalties—of Chad's duty.

Strether has to ponder not only the question but "the sore abysses it revealed" before he can bravely answer, "Of course they're totally different sorts of duty"—an abstract reply which might be intelligible to the New England mind were it not followed by an affronting explication to the effect that Strether's state of mind, and, by polite if not ironic inclusion, pre-European Sarah's, proceeded from "our queer New England ignorance, our queer misconceptions and confusions—from which, since then, an inexorable tide of light seems to have floated us into our perhaps still queerer knowledge."

Sarah and party leave indignantly and virtuously for the Alps, and Strether faces, in Book XI, a new trial of conscience and consciousness. He has had earlier adjustments to make—for eminent example that it is the married mother and not her daughter with whom Chad is in love. Yet he has been sustained by a formula which he has been careful not to test too rigorously—little Bilham's formula that what was under scrutiny was "an innocent attachment." Now he is called upon to witness not indeed the act of adultery but a situation which can scarcely be interpreted by easy inference as other, and his consciousness is forced to admit both that the relationship between Chad and Mme de Vionnet has never been purely 'spiritual' and yet that little Bilham's delicate ambiguity of an "innocent attachment" was, in a sense which he can no longer deny, true. If there can be a conflict between duties, so there can be a distinction between sexual relations—a point made, to Anglo-Saxon distress, by Swedenborg in his book *Conjugal Love*.

Mme de Vionnet does her subtle best at face-saving,

not for her sake or Chad's but for Strether's; yet he is left with three pains: the "quantity of make-believe involved, and so vividly exemplified" that it violently disagrees with his "spiritual stomach"; and (in one of those "vain vigils," those sleepless nights, so often attributed to 'poor Strether') the pity that the make-belief should be "so much like lying"; and, lastly, the contrast the revealed intimacy of these others makes to his own cold loneliness.

Now Strether's conscience has been educated, stretched, as far as it can go. He has learned to distinguish, in the case of others, tints and shades between white and black. And to this new-found ability to distinguish—or to admit to his consciousness that he can distinguish—he has sacrificed his chance of returning to Woollett, his marriage to Mrs. Newsome, his thus acquired economic security, although perhaps the first two were not severe losses but partly releases. Miss Gostrey must test out whether his knowledge of the "virtuous attachment" 's real nature, a knowledge she had all along possessed but felt he was conceivably not ready to take, has made an arrest of his independence. . . , a revulsion in favor of the principles of Woollett"; she discovers it has not. He has arrived at one of the latest refinements of the New England conscience: that one can charitably allow others to do what one wouldn't do oneself, or, to put it another way, that one's public conscience is emancipated beyond one's private.

There are no very credible reasons why Strether must return to New England. Chad would doubtless support him; Maria Gostrey wants to marry him, and in her he would have a sympathetic and intelligent companion. This rejection of Miss Gostrey is not eased for the reader by James's calling her the novel's *ficelle;* and Strether's rejection of her proposal—Strether must always be proposed to—certainly appears—if one wants to phrase it so—as failure to do a duty. But still Strether must return. The only reason he can give Maria is that he must go "to be right" and that "to be right" is, "out of the whole affair, not to have got anything for myself."

The last scenes with both Mme de Vionnet and Miss Gostrey are masterly in the women's shrewd appraisals of Strether. According to the former, to feel himself victimized is evidently the way he must live. The latter reminds him that he has got something for himself—his "wonderful impressions"—but when reminded that he has not got, because he has not asked for, her, charmingly asks, "But why should you be so dreadfully right?"

James manages to shift the emphasis in the final lines of dialogue by having Miss Gostrey pun on the word *right.* In her question, *right* means *good*, and *good* means *self-sacrificing;* in her final and as James calls it her "defeated protest," the word shifts its meaning to 'true to type.' "It isn't so much you're being 'right'—it's your horrible sharp eye for what makes you so."

Yet Miss Gostrey's question remains—Why does Strether have to be so "dreadfully right"? And perhaps not less than her comment. Strether's emancipated conscience in judging others, an emancipation painful to him in the process and hardly joyful in the end, has still left him pride—his pride in the supererogatory rigors of his own, his New England, conscience.

MARY E. WILKINS
(1852–1930)

Miss Wilkins was a native of Randolph, Massachusetts, fourteen miles south of Boston. Though she lived for some years in Brattleboro, Vermont (and, after her marriage to Dr. Charles Freeman, for some further years in Metuchen, New Jersey), it is primarily Randolph which shaped her creative mind.

Randolph belongs—or belonged—to Massachusetts' shoe factory area. It was once larger than Brockton. When Miss Wilkins was born, much of the work on shoes, especially "cording" them, was carried on, sometimes by women, in small sheds standing by the shoemakers' houses.

After the Civil War, New England began its decline. The railroads across the continent were built. Enterprising young men, following Horace Greeley's advice, "went West"; the village system of home industry, small farming, chiefly 'subsistence farming,' began to break down. And though the white Congregational church still stood on one side of the village green, the clergy were no longer content, like those of the seventeenth and eighteenth centuries, to be life-long pastors of a country parish. The ministers of Miss Wilkins' villages are either young men just out of theological school or commonplace aging men awaiting retirement.

In a Wilkins village, the women—widows and spinsters—outnumber the men: a young woman has to think three times before she rejects an offer of marriage. And the men, such as they are, are weaker than the women: less determined of character, less sharply defined. The older women—many if not most of them—are what New England calls 'characters.' They are mostly genteelly poor. Think of the huge meals Dickens' people eat, and then of the supper in a Wilkins' lady's cottage: some thinly sliced white bread, a glass saucer of currants, a pot of tea. The Babcock sisters (in "A Gala Dress") lack even the saucer of currants, or its equivalent; and "No sauce for tea was regarded as very poor living by the village women." To have an egg is a luxury. Cruder folk (like men and Matilda Jennings—also in "A Gala Dress") may have salt pork, cold potatoes, baked beans, or mackerel. But these are concessions to the flesh.

The Wilkins people have all been "brought up on the rigid New England plan"—the one I not only remember but feel. It *seemed absolute morality;* it was actually, I can take in, though I but imperfectly feel it, only *a morality:* one which antedated even the approach to the Socialized State ('social security' and the like) which the United States had reached by 1965. According to the "rigid New England plan," a mortgage is an immorality;

buying anything on 'the installment plan' is immoral: one shouldn't buy anything until he can pay the full price in 'ready money.' Increasing one's income by investment (however conservative) in stocks and bonds is immoral. Perhaps the most solemn injunction of this now archaic New England morality is that it is immoral "to be beholden" to anyone. Loans, gifts, and charity are not to be accepted. What one can't pay for in cash or reciprocity of services rendered (estimated in terms of time and money), one goes without: "I have my pride."

Pride: how ambivalent that quality is among the genteel poor. In that context it can hardly be called a great splendid 'deadly sin.' Without it Miss Wilkins' women would lose their desire to live, their psychic *structure*. It may be founded on faint distinctions and on the slight eminences, social, mental and artistic (the "Village Singer," the village "Poetess," the "Old Arithmetician," who, having a "faculty" and "gift" for ciphering, solves a sum the young male high-school teacher can't solve); the pride of the "Independent Thinker," who, too deaf to hear the sermon, doesn't go to church but works defiantly at her knitting, the proceeds from which go, anonymously, to help the very neighbor who censures her for not keeping the Sabbath; but fundamentally it seems a willingness to suffer for nonconformity to standards which one cannot accept.

This is an 'Orthodox' community in the New England sense: there is no Unitarian Church which has, legally, stolen the white meetinghouse on the green and the communion silver. The old ladies, whether they 'go to meeting' or not, read a chapter in the Bible before bedtime. The Ten Commandments are as real as the New England rocks and hills: especially, thou shalt not steal; thou shalt not covet thy neighbor's goods; thou shalt not bear false witness; honor thy father and thy mother, and more especially thy mother.

As the 'bed-rock' beneath any such specificities is the First and Greatest Commandment, Thou Ought. It's your Duty. How charmingly ingenuous and supernaturally innocent is that quatrain of Emerson's learned at 'school':

> So nigh is grandeur to our dust
> So near is God to man
> When Duty whispers low, 'Thou must',
> The youth replies, 'I can'.

Easy for Emerson; but how hard for the battered and worn, who hesitatingly say, "It's my Dooty and I must do it," or who, like Ann Millet (a cat her only "Object of Love"), say its ritual equivalent.

As Ann looks at her squashes (upon which she and her pussy cat, Willy, feed), she says to herself, " 'A splendid lot they *air* . . . I'd *orter to be thankful.*' " "Ann always spoke of her *obligation to duty*"—her duty to duty—"and never seemed to think of herself as performing the duty itself. 'I'd *orter* be thankful', said she always."

I have written of nonconformist pride, the pride of what, in the title of one of her stories, Miss Wilkins calls the "Independent Thinker." In its own way, this is the Thoreauvian pride at "signing off" from a society, or the rules of a society, which one does not accept. It seems to say, "Every man *ought to be* an island to himself"—or perhaps we should add, a mountain, or at least a hill. Emerson says—so elegantly and urbanely that the bark *and bite* may be missed—"We *descend to meet*"—one of those half-truths salutary in certain contexts. But this fine utterance is perhaps less true than the opposite half-truth, that we ascend to meet: we put on our best Sunday clothes and try to behave and think and talk better than our solitary routine.

A friend used to say to me when we were both young, "Only the strong can love the strong"; and his axiom much impressed me. One can argue, of course, that strength is not all of the same kind; and in real friendship or real marriage one of the partners is strong in one way and the other in another: they pool their strengths.

But, on the whole, I have no wish to argue or to subtilize. We must be selves, possessed of a proper degree of self-love and self-respect, before we can, in any real way, love others. You must have a self before you can give it away. To a neurotic, Jesus' saying, "Thou shalt love thy neighbor as thyself," is high, lofty, and so on but baffling—because one can't love oneself with that normal degree of self-love and self-respect which the injunction seems to presuppose.

'Neurotic pride' (which keeps people going but which also isolates them) has, finally, to be broken down—if not through a "breakdown" through a public confession. Secret penance is inadequate. Penitence—a different thing—involves confession to the one we have wronged, either to the wronged one or, ideally, to the community, and involves restitution. A wrong we have done is not only a 'sin against God' and a wrong against our particular neighbor but a wrong against society, or community, that which constitutes an organic continuum between the individual and God. Touching examples drawn from Miss Wilkins' tales are "A Stolen Christmas," "Calla-Lilies and Hannah" (with confession before the church congregation), and "Sister Liddy" (who, dying in the almshouse, has to confess that, not having once 'had' and now 'lost' 'things'—having no past glories or connections about which to boast—she has invented the sister upon whose surpassing grandeur she has dilated to her fellow inmates).

Something approximating a majority of Miss Wilkins' stories seem to me to deal with 'cases of conscience'—that is, with situations in which the protagonist is confronted with principles or duties which present rival claims. As—in latter-day Protestantism at least—one can tell what one's duty is by its giving neither pleasure or joy, but, at the most, a kind of grim self-approbation—it is fair to say that Wilkins women do not always recognize that they are confronted with 'rival duties'—though a Jesuit or an Anglican like Bishop Jeremy Taylor or Bishop Kirk would certainly say that they were. Self-fulfillment is—if abstractly put—as much a duty as 'self-sacrifice.' It is as much a duty to receive—especially with grateful grace—as it is to give (something often done in New England with such absence of tenderness or delicacy that one would be grateful indeed not to have to be "beholden").

The habitual problems of conscience for fairly decent people less concern the "struggle between good and evil"—or virtue and sin—than they do that of finding, in a particular case, which good principle should be allowed precedence over which other good principle. And as for "sin"—the practical problem (as the 'permissive' psychiatrist, at least, knows—and doubtless the wise and generous priest as well) is that if one can't keep every jot and tittle of the Law (and who can?) it is better to commit the venial rather than the 'mortal' or 'deadly' sin. Your principles, to be sure, ought to be clear, but your application of them should be flexible.

But, as Anglican Bishop Kirk's *Conscience and Its Problems* should make clear—not, indeed, to the subtle and sinuous though entirely sincere John Henry Newman, who wouldn't need it, but to his manly and muscularly Christian opponent, Charles Kingsley—the province of casuistry rightly understood, is coterminous with practical ethics (that is, the adjustment of collisions between *duties;* the sensible and sensitive judgment of how to apply more or less permanent 'principles' to 'situations' or 'cases' which constantly vary).

Most of Henry James's short stories and *novellas* deal with 'cases of conscience,' but with such cases as exist at relatively high social, intellectual, and moral altitudes. Miss Wilkins' stories, which deal with the 'genteel poor' and 'humble folk,' show that casuistry has no social or intellectual limitation to its scope.

Perhaps these 'cases' (what might, more simply, be called 'moral problems') are—like psychiatric treatment—easier to manage with people of a relatively high intelligence—and with a clergyman or an equivalent person of relatively high intelligence and intuition: it is notable that the Protestant clergymen in Miss Wilkins' tales are practically useless as analysts and counsellors. But over this 'perhaps' I hesitate, knowing all the ways that intelligence can avoid and evade the simplest moral obligations; how you can be too smart for your own good, and too brilliant to be wise,—knowing also that the counsellor need not be more brilliant than the counselled, but must be more steadfast, more balanced, more centered.

The fact remains that Wilkins people have little guidance from without. They are all Bible readers; but they certainly show the comparative uselessness of Bible-reading unaccompanied by interpretative theology,—Bible-reading, that is, of texts read uncontextually. It seems that—as with the ancestral New England Puritans who landed on "the stern and rockbound coast"—it is the Old

Testament rather than the New, the Law rather than the Gospel, which, chiefly, they have understood. And it follows, I think, that in the 'cases of conscience' Miss Wilkins gives us, it is often a struggle between the authority of the Old Testament (as her people understand it) and something they don't think of as 'religious' at all—the voice of common sense, the voice of private conscience, the voice of 'charity'—that is, of love.

Apposite is the story "Gentian," told almost entirely from the point of view of Lucy Tollet, the elderly wife of Alfred Tollet. "Alferd," the household autocrat, has all his life been very healthy; but now, all spring, he complains of "great depression and languor" and has not attempted to work in his garden. His wife can't induce him to see a doctor; as she tells her sister, "Alferd was allus jest so. He ain't never thought nothin' of doctors, nor doctors' stuff."

Lucy's unmarried sister, to whom she reports, has her own brand of impatience with "Alferd" and theories. If he won't see a doctor, he should certainly be made to "take somethin' "—"Somethin' bitter"—probably gentian. Says sister Hannah, "I'd make him, ef I put it in his tea unbeknownst to him"; and Hannah continues, "I don't *believe in deceivin' generally*, but I don't believe the Lord would hev let folk hed the *faculty* for deceivin' in 'em ef it wan't to be used fur good sometimes."

Lucy takes Hannah's advice—only, as "Alferd" complains of the tea tasting bitter, she takes to putting little sprinklings of it in the bread, pies, and everything she cooks. And Alfred immediately begins to be better, and by September is as hearty as ever. "But his wife seemed to lose as he gained. . . . She did *not go to church at all*, and she had been a devout church-goer."

Lucy is unable to take, with 'good conscience,' the

sister's casuistical advice upon which, with results so beneficial to her old husband, she has acted. And finally she bursts out in confession to her sister: "I deceived him, an' it's been 'most killin' me to think on't ever since." And then Lucy feels compelled to confess to her husband—whereupon, first, he will eat nothing she cooks, and, shortly after, he allows her to go to live with her sister.

The ending of the story is perhaps here irrelevant—though it is psychologically sound to New England character. After a separation of autumn and winter, Lucy visits her own house and begs her husband, standing there with his hat, to let her return. He sends her back to her sister's, though with a new tone in his voice. In a few minutes her husband appears, obstinate in carrying out his ritual idea that it is he who should confess and beg forgiveness. "I've come to ask you to come home, Lucy. I'm a-feelin' kinder poorly this spring, an'—I want you ter stew me up a little gentian. What you give me afore did me a sight of good." Certainly, the love behind it, the love which prompted Lucy to do something so contrary to her conscience as to deceive—that love had done him "a world of good."

Pride can easily beget solitude: one isn't willing to bow to one's superiors, nor associate with one's inferiors; and—in a village, at least, with its small distinctions of eminence and lowness—it is difficult to think of others who are admitted to be one's equals. This is not to say that solitude begets pride; but that, too, is a 'genealogy of morals' which could be illustrated out of Helen Waddell's wonderful *Desert Fathers*, the early Christian hermits of Egypt.

There is an extraordinary short story of Miss Wilkins which I long overlooked—perhaps because of its deviation from type. It is about an isolated *man;* and its 'chorus' is not that of village women but of that 'club' of rural philosophers and yarn-spinners who make the 'general store' their headquarters; and it comes nearer to the explicitness of a 'moral' than any other I can remember—a 'moral' not merely of this story but of all the stories one could tell, whether about New England or India.

For six years, Nicholas Gunn, once married, has lived alone in an unheated cabin distant from the village. During a snowstorm, he sits at his open door, as "calmly passive . . . as a Buddhist monk." He leads a thoroughly ascetic life. Though he has a stove, he makes himself eat his hasty pudding cold. Though he has a cot bed, he sleeps "rolled in a blanket, on the bare floor." He reads his Bible by the light of a candle. Whatever the cause of his eccentricities—whether "mystical religious fervor" or "his own personal sorrows, [he] would have been revered and worshipped as a saintly ascetic among some nations." But in his native New England, he was ridiculed as either a "darned fool" or "cracked."

Reiterated circumstance forces his conscience to take in—to adopt—a feeble and consumptive old peddler whose half-sister is going to commit him to the poor farm.

The reluctant host tries to explain how he became an ascetic. Having had "lots of trouble," "mainly through folks I set by," he had figured out that if he didn't care anything for anybody he wouldn't have trouble from them, and if he didn't care anything about himself he wouldn't have any trouble from that quarter. "I kept cold when I wanted to be warm, an' warm when I wanted to be cold. I didn't eat anything I liked, an' I left things around that hurt me to see." He read the

Bible because he no longer believed in it, and so reading it made him feel worse. "I did about everything I could to spite myself an' get all the feelin' out of me. . . ."

But now the ex-hermit sees that his solution was wrong, though he expresses his change of mind in a characteristically New England way, a negatively toned version of Margaret Fuller's exuberant, conceited, and un-New England declaration—her "I accept the universe." Nicholas Gunn says of the 'world,' of life, with its unpredictable anxieties and pains, "I've got to go through with the whole of it *like other folks*, an' I guess I've got grit enough. I've made up my mind that men's tracks cover the whole world, and there ain't standin'-room outside of 'em. I've got to go with the rest."

Miss Wilkins does not spoil the ending of the story, despite two closing paragraphs which give a mildly poetic and symbolic sign that a 'conversion experience' has taken place. She keeps her balance steady by a maxim of her own, less picturesque and more abstract than Gunn's speech. His guest, she says, "did not in the least understand him, *but that did not matter*. There is a *higher*"—delightful substitute for the expected *lower*—or even *deeper*—"There is a higher congeniality than that of mutual understanding; there is that of need and supply."

Miss Wilkins' stories are not autobiographical. She wrote the best of them while she was a spinster, yet not (like her *New England Nun*) vowed by her habits to celibacy, only waiting—waiting, in her case, till she married in her late forties the handsome Dr. Freeman of Metuchen, New Jersey. Her family were genteelly poor Congregationalists; and she wrote to support herself, not primarily to be 'creative,' as Sarah Orne Jewett professed to do, or to defend village people ('the natives,' as they were called in my youth) against the patronage of 'summer boarders.' Yet she had the conscience of a literary craftsman. Her stories have neither extraneous descriptive passages exhibiting her own sensibility nor passages (such as Mrs. Stowe, in her exuberance, poured out) explaining the New England character or expositing its theologies. There are few words, let alone sentences, which one would like to cross out as 'redundant.' She is spare and stripped, like Maupassant, whom she surely read, and the later Tolstoi, for whose "Three Lives" she expressed admiration. Best of all, in contrast to the Miss Jewett of *Country of the Pointed Firs,* Miss Wilkins does not tell her tales from the point of view of a city visitor, however sympathetic, nor swathe the dialogue of her characters in her own prose: her stories are almost entirely told in dialogue.

Her literary objectivity may have been helped by her own unromantic character. To one woman friend she deeply cared about, she wrote—in an undated but fairly early letter, "You are fond of people, and I never have been." In the sense she meant it, this was always true of her: she was *interested* by people and their motives—as devoid of hostility or satire as of "fondness." And this extended into something even rarer: she could view herself and own life and the ups and downs of her 'bachelor days' and her not particularly fortunate marriage as though they all belonged to somebody else.

As for her personal involvement in the ethical rigorism and scrupulosity she so often narratively described, the best testimony is a letter she wrote about her year at Mount Holyoke in 1870, twenty years after the death of Mary Lyon, its celebrated founder, under whom Emily Dickinson suffered and stood her own ground: "As I remember, I did not behave as well at Mount

Holyoke; and I am inclined to attribute it to monotony of diet and *too strenuous goadings* of conscience."

Miss Wilkins' mind, like that of Henry James (who read her first two and best collections with admiration), was not "violated by ideas." She was neither a rebel against New England orthodoxy nor a belated and belligerent advocate of it. Nicholas Gunn's speech in "A Solitary," negative and cautious as it is, is singularly abstract for her, who was—strange to say of one who, at a certain level, knew New England so well—not at all a theoretician. If her common sense and moderation are not more quickly observed, it is because her nature was so much that of an artist that she can glow with the aberrations—understood but scarcely shared—of her characters.

HENRY ADAMS
(1838–1918)

The *Education of Henry Adams* was written in 1905. Adams liked to say, half in jest, that his great ambition was to complete St. Augustine's *Confessions:* the Saint having worked from multiplicity to unity—he, from unity to multiplicity.

How does this remarkable, difficult book contribute to a study of the New England conscience? 'Conscience,' neither as word or concept, is writ large in Adams' book, yet it is there—one is tempted to say as 'consciousness' (the same word has to serve for moral vigilance and every other kind in French—*conscience*). One can begin by saying that it is a New Englander's *duty* to be ever conscious—never to allow himself to fall into torpor, lethargy, or the opiate of 'light reading.' Whether one's life is painful or not, his duty is to sit bolt upright and to keep his eyes open.

That 'conscience' is not a word which often appears in Adams' book is chiefly, I think, due to the fact he seems never to have been conscious of *sinning*. He was reared in that period in which, near Boston, 'sinning' had disappeared. "Nothing quieted doubt so completely as the mental calm of the Unitarian clergy. In uniform excellence of life and character, moral and intellectual, the score of Unitarian clergy, who controlled society and Harvard College, were never excelled"—a remark only half-ironical, I think.

But there are reminders and maxims of conscience. There is the maxim of William M. Evarts, the friend of that Dana who was two years "before the mast," but who was a man of great refinement trying to harden himself: "I pride myself on my success in doing not the things I like to do, but the things I don't like to do"—a pride at once Puritan and Kantian.

Then there is Adams' description of himself as a boy: "The habit of doubt; of distrusting his own judgment *and* of totally rejecting the judgment of the world;... the passion for companionship and the antipathy to society—all these are well-known qualities of New England character." And there is the generalization, taken from the very first chapter: "Resistance to something was the law of New England nature;... for numberless generations his predecessors had viewed the world chiefly as a thing to be reformed, filled with evil forces to be abolished, and they saw no reason to suppose that they had wholly succeeded in the abolition...; the New Englander, whether boy or man, in his long struggle with a stingy or hostile universe, had learned also to love the pleasure of hating... one's self if no better victim offered...."

But there are new notes which come into this book of

Adams, and that is the reason why he must come into this book. The seventeenth-century Puritans tried to set up a Holy Commonwealth from which all unbelievers would be excluded. And Adams knew in his boyhood his grandfather, John Quincy Adams, who, defeated for a second term as President, accepted the humble office of representing the farmers of Plymouth County in Congress, on the Burkean condition that he should never have to campaign for election and that, if elected, he would vote and say what he, not they, thought right. Elected, he remained in Congress from 1831 till his death in 1848, perhaps the last career of its kind in these United States.

"The Irish gardener once said to the child [Henry]: 'You'll be thinkin' you'll be President too.'" And to Henry, as a child, that seemed natural. But the days of 'oligarchy' were over. Henry's father, Charles Francis, was ambassador to England during the Civil War. Henry and his erratic but certainly brilliant brother Brooks never rose higher than to be professors. Henry was assistant professor of history at Harvard from 1871–77, seven years, under that strange, shrewd, ambitious, well-intentioned President Eliot. The chapter on Adams' professorship is entitled "Failure." Why did he think teaching any more of a failure that any of the things he did in a long life?

Partly, doubtless, because 'history,' like 'English,' is one of those vague, amorphic subjects which—after a fashion, and to the satisfaction of most 'students'—any one can teach. Adams' *intellectual conscience*, never extinguished by any amount of irony he poured on it, could scarcely be satisfied. "A teacher must either treat history as a catalogue, a record, a romance, or as an evolution; and whether he affirms or denies evolution, he falls into all the burning faggots of the pit. . . . In essence incoherent and immoral, history had either to be taught as such [that is, as incoherent and immoral]—or falsified. Adams wanted to do neither. He had no theory of evolution to teach and could not make the facts fit one." By 'evolution' I understand Adams to mean 'philosophy of history': some causal sequence, not necessarily 'the idea of progress.' The 'Middle Ages' assigned him were the something like a thousand years between ancient history and modern history; and it seemed to Adams, as a young assistant professor as it did later, that the thousand years should be, as no one since Gibbon had attempted, attached intelligibly to the 'before' anl 'after'; yet "history had nowhere broken down, so pitiably, or avowed itself so hopelessly bankrupt" as in knowing how to do this.

Adams, intent on his own education, was too honest not to want, paid as professor, to educate his students, but he was not satisfied that he could. He didn't believe in the German—and Eliotic—lecture system. "No man can instruct more than half-a-dozen students at once. The whole problem of education is one of its cost in money." These maxims, thrown out in passing, though in need of explanation, are certainly more than half true. Another is worth quoting for its own sake as well as for Adams, who, like most men who have had a formal education, think, rightly or wrongly, that they learned little from it: Out of ten Harvard men, "nine in ten take polish passively, like a hard surface; only the tenth sensibly reacts. Adams thought that, as no one seemed to care what he did, he would try to cultivate this tenth mind, though necessarily at the expense of the other nine."

A 'sensible' American would say, when Adams thought himself a failure as a professor, and had scarcely a good word for Harvard under the great Eliot, that Adams was of course thinking of 'formal education' as training in method of thinking. In large measure this was true. Adams asked one of his students, whose "faith in education was so full of pathos," what he could do with his 'education' after he had got it, and was told, "The degree of Harvard College is worth money to me in Chicago." This was in the 1870's; yet probably the answer would not be very different now. But need 'formal education' be so separated from that kind of life-long education, which was Adams' goal, is the subject of his book, and is, to speak philosophically and theologically, the true life of man here and hereafter?

There is, of course—for men as for women—the education which is all most Americans want, perhaps—education "worth money in Chicago," education which trains one for a profession, or the education which gives polish—the 'finishing school'. How can you find, and by what method can you educate, the "tenth man" who "sensibly reacts"? Psychiatrists want to teach the neurotics how to 'adjust themselves to society.' West Point—and its equivalents—want to train a young soldier according to the methods which won the last war. But what if society ought to be altered? What if the next war will be fought and won by new rules, new tactics? Questions of this sort lie behind Adams' doubts of formal education (the advantage of having which is, of course, to know one hasn't failed because he never went to Oxford or Harvard) and his bafflement about how one gets a *real* education.

What he means one can define only by inference. He was fond of thinking himself born in the wrong century: he was an eighteenth-century child; perhaps, with more strength of the imagination, a thirteenth-century child; perhaps he could have been a child of the twenty-first century. Religion, as it had been understood before, after, elsewhere had disappeared; yet it seemed to him in later life that religion was, next to the sexual, "the most *powerful* emotion of man," and not 'emotion' merely as something 'given': as educatable and educative. So, too, were the arts and aesthetic experience and, not less, social experience—a social experience not limited to Boston.

But what is education, however broadly conceived, to be education for? Adams seems clear about that: education is for power, not ornamentation. The three generations of Adamses before him—the two Presidents and his father, American ambassador to England—had been men who all along with, or should one say despite, their general culture, had wielded political power, social power. Henry felt certainly, and keenly, the degradation from being a maker of history to being—however able—a professor of history and a writer of history, and—what he was least competent at—a philosopher of history.

He did not willingly accept this inferior role—that of interpreter. After the Civil War, Boston gradually shrank to a secondary position in literature and politics, a museum and a shrine. In 1888 the novelist Howells moved from Boston to New York, now the American literary center. Anticipating his move by a year, Adams, who in 1872 had married Marian Hooper, moved to Washington, which, he wrote his closest British friend, Charles Milnes Gaskell, is "this only place in America where society amuses me, or where life offers variety." He was not wholly frank in another sentence from his letter to Gaskell, "As I am intimate with many of the people in power and out of power, I am readily allowed or aided to do all the historical work I please; and as I am avowedly out of politics, there will be, it is hoped, no animosities to meet."

All of this statement is literally true; but its implications are not. He chose the most central place in which to study American politics and politicians in action. But Adams meant also to be where, entertained and entertaining, he would be accessible to what still, in 1965, is called being 'drafted'—a notion which, in our time, except perhaps for General Eisenhower, is a fiction—that of the man who, without making any overt action or spending any money, is *called* to the service of his country—as Adams' grandfather had been called by the voters of Plymouth County to represent them in Congress. Adams certainly never expected to be 'drafted' for the presidency. But, with his experience and training, he had, doubtless, some right to expect a reasonably imperative request for his services as cabinet member or ambassador. Such a request never came. "Every friend in power is a friend lost" is one of his maxims. In 1892, he wrote: "Why had no President ever cared to employ him?"

Even the watching of American politics became partly baffling, distasteful, even perhaps disgusting, to a man of social conscience and integrity. The palpable, the overt, degradation began with the administration of Grant—who, strange to relate, seemed on voting day, to Adams as to four-fifths of the American people—a partial parallel to Washington—a great soldier who, as such, represented order. The disillusionment was catastrophic. Grant reminded him of Garibaldi: "In both, the intellect counted for nothing; only the energy counted. The type was pre-intellectual, archaic, and would have seemed so even to cave-dwellers." In 1869 occurred the famous attempt of Jay Gould to corner gold, on the supposition that under Grant's administration, and with Grant's brother-in-law's complicity, he could do this without interference from the government. Adams and his brother went to New York, interviewed Gould's *âme damnée,* Jim Fisk; Henry wrote up the story, published in the English *Westminster Review.*

"The newspapers discussed little else than the alleged moral laxity of Grant, Garfield, and Blaine," and "some of Adams' best friends, like Godkin [editor of *The Nation*] ruined their influence by their insistence on points of morals." But, so it seemed, "The moral law had expired,—like the Constitution." "Practical Americans laughed and went their way. . . . Every hope or thought which brought Adams to Washington proved to be absurd. No one wanted him; no one wanted any of his *friends in reform;* the *blackmailer alone was the normal product of politics as of business.*"

In 1893 Adams formed a friendship with Senator Cameron of Pennsylvania. "The Camerons had what the Adamses thought the political way of reaching their objects without much regard to their methods"—by which, as he develops the theme, Adams seems to mean that the Camerons—the Pennsylvania politicians—thought the ends justified the means; while "more than silver and gold, the moral standard interested Adams." Yet he saw that one law ruled all others—"the masses of men follow interest in deciding morals. Morality is a private and costly luxury"—without accepting either communism or Catholicism, both of which had their mild attraction for him. The nearest he could ever come to a political label was the confessedly paradoxical and obviously whimsical "Conservative Christian Anarchist," the 'party' of two or three members which his young friends Bay Lodge and Joe Stickney had devised.

Adams died at eighty, still trying to learn. His legacy in the form of philosophy of history seems to me neither final nor impressive. The last two, the famous two, books are *Mont-Saint-Michel and Chartres: a Study of Thirteenth-Century Unity;* and *The Education: a Study of Twentieth-Century Multiplicity;* and both periods, he thought, might be studied at once in philosophy and mechanics. But the mind is incapable of satisfaction in chaos, and Adams—at least in old age—couldn't master enough physical science (mathematics and physics in particular) to discover the unity which lay beyond twentieth-century multiplicity.

Nor is his famous antithesis of the Virgin, the Force which created thirteenth-century civilization, and the Dynamo, corresponding force of the twentieth century, an antithesis which can well be borne down upon. The two symbols, so to say, are not parallel. Men did once worship the Virgin, as a theological person who answered prayer, gave favors; men do not worship the dynamo in any corresponding sense. They value and desire the gadgets and effects of steam, gas, and electricity. The Virgin is a 'First Cause'; the products of the dynamo are 'material causes.'

But there is something in Adams' thinking here which is never clarified. Perhaps because of his wife's death, which divided his life in halves, the second half of his life is an exaltation of Woman—Venus, the Virgin, the American woman of the nineteenth century. Any one "brought up among Puritans knew that sex was Sin. In any previous age, sex was strength.... Every one, even among Puritans, knew that neither Diana of the Ephesians nor any of the Oriental goddesses was worshipped for her beauty. She was goddess because of her force; she was the *animated dynamo;* she was reproduction—the greatest and most mysterious of all energies; all she needed was to be fecund." Not one of Adams' educators, he says, had called his attention to the opening lines of Lucretius, "perhaps the finest in all Latin literature, where the poet invoked Venus exactly as Dante invoked the Virgin:

'Quae quoniam rerum naturam *sola* gubernas.' "

What is the 'lesson' of Henry Adams? The lesson of an 'intellectual' never satisfied with his intellectual achievements or what he knew, one whose education was never completed and never could be completed. His was not primarily a *personal moral* conscience. Even in *The Education*, I find little self-analysis and that of an elementary sort. Much analysis there is, and that of an acute variety—at its best in Chapters VII through XI, given to the English statesmen's attitudes and actions during the American Civil War: analysis of the intellectual and moral characters of Palmerston, Russell, Gladstone, their motivations and their utterances. As Adams says, in his chapter called "Political Morality," "Henry James had not yet [1862] taught the world to read a volume for the pleasure of seeing the lights of his burning-glass turned on alternate sides of the same figure." Young Adams, and his father, Charles Francis, had to teach themselves; and young Adams lived to be old enough to read the official 'life and letters' of each of the British statesmen and find that both he and his father had quite misjudged the men they dealt with.

What is the 'lesson' of Henry Adams and his conscience? Whatever he might fancy he would have liked to be, his vocation was that of a scholar—a scholar, one can fairly say, on something like the universal lines of Leibniz or the French Encylopedists—not to risk names more recent. He wanted an honest American polity, but, more or less despairing of that, he wanted at any event to know the 'behind the scenes' mechanism of Federal polity—of which he presents a bitter picture in his novel, *Democracy*. He was never content with slogans, pious commonplaces, unsupported and unexamined generalizations. If he spent seven years 'teaching "history" ' and wrote a nine-volume history of two early nineteenth-century American adminstrations, he wanted, with equal accuracy and relentlessness, to know his own time. But that did not content him. 'History' is a loose concept; but, if it is to be other, one must seek to make himself a philosopher of history. What, precisely, do you mean by 'history'?

I see the intellectual conscience of Adams as beginning, where it should begin, with one's private history —with the Adams family and Quincy and Boston and New England, then moving on and outward to the ever-larger questions—which are, indeed, really involved even when one deals with the seemingly nearest and most particular concerns. The dialectic relation between the smallest 'fact' and the most grandiose generalization can never be overcome.

Adams never quite says this: I can offer no ready 'proof-text.' But it is implicit in his work. Nor does he ever say—or quite see—the two almost universally disjunct characters of the researcher (the antiquarian, the fact-finder) and the interpreter and philosopher of history—this doubtless because, like his favorite historian, Gibbon, he had the leisure and the talent for both. Each of these two characters (poles, really) requires conscientiousness of intellect: the scholar must be sure that his 'facts' are 'facts'; the interpreter must be sure that there are no relevant facts with which he has not dealt, and sure that his generalizations are not merely rhetorical and that the evidence on which he bases them is clearly indicated.

Adams died with his education still incomplete. Complete it could never be, if only because it was a New England conscience which was to be educated. But, in the declining years of that conscience, he is a figure of honor. Though he reached no solutions which permanently satisfied him—or us, he went on asking questions, and those questions were central ones, for they concerned Sex, Politics; the State, the Individual; Art, Science; Power, Integrity.

EDWIN ARLINGTON ROBINSON
(1869–1935)

Robinson's 'case' is near enough to my own time so that I can understand its complexity. He came, not from Boston or Massachusetts but from the 'State of Maine,' out of a family and friends who were in some real sense 'gone to seed,' 'run out,' living in a sparsely populated state agreeably inhabited for perhaps three summer months.

And his central 'personal' problem is a New Englandly familiar one: he never could make his peace between wanting to be respectable (a money maker and keeper, moderately orthodox in church and 'Americanism') and his necessity (expressed in a bleak New England way) to be a poet ("I don't know how to be anything else")—still, in New England, outside, perhaps, of Boston, not a man's job. Though he naturally had much of the time to consort with them, Robinson was not a real 'Bohemian.' For a moment, perhaps, when his *Tristram* won a Pulitzer prize, he could feel mild comfort; but he could never, like Frost (Amy Lowell's *Recent Tendencies in American Poetry* probably started the coupling, based on little more than the fact that both were New England poets), 'sell' himself. He couldn't lecture or read his poetry before an audience; he couldn't, like Frost, assume the role of rusticity; he couldn't write or lecture *about* poetry; he had none of Frost's gregariousness; and, finally, unlike Frost, he had no 'homely wisdom' to impart and no lyrical lyrics to sing.

He was so bleak, that I (who once saw him—not on a lecture platform but in one of those desolate white-tiled lunchrooms near Copley Square—sitting, in almost complete silence with an old Boston journalist friend, another 'failure') wondered, as I used to when I read his poetry, why, no religious scruples or faiths preventing, he didn't commit suicide. Nor can I flippantly say 'that would be too easy and melodramatic,' though both are true. 'Stoicism' would also be too easy. I venture that his conscience (of a decadent New England variety) made him derive a kind of negative pleasure out of *enduring*, a bony toughness. "Whatever else we were put here on earth for, it wasn't to be happy." This folk saying (neither Robinson's nor of New England) I think of when I think of Robinson; and I can quote it because, though theological presuppositions lie behind it, they are not overt.

There is something so latter-day Yankee about Robinson. He could not but respect Yankee thrift, belief in work, belief that he who works hard will prosper, and all the rest. He could neither denounce them nor, himself, practice them, save in a translated form which, he was conscious, his fellow countrymen would not recognize. He could never get completely the better of his boyhood feelings of being a failure by those Yankee standards which, though he could not accept them for himself, he could not reject them *in general*—as being, for most people, sound.

So he was one kind of *divided man*. If, at thirty or thirty-five, say, he had achieved 'success' (money and fame), recognized as such by the newspapers of Gardiner, Maine, he might, perhaps, have become a different man. He didn't. His 'fame' was bestowed too late and too grudgingly; his money was never enough. And whatever he may have read about the princely patrons of 'artists' in the Renaissance and later, he must have found it painful—a sign of failure, not worth—to be meagerly supported for years by a *group* of patrons.

It is natural that with part of him he fought back against Yankee standards with his early long poems like *Captain Craig*, that he adopted and never wholly relinquished the paradox (ultimately Christian) according to which 'success' is failure, and failure may well be victory, salvation. The Puritans, like the Methodists—like so many religious-minded groups—may have started with this view, but it proves hard to sustain after the first ardors and martyrdoms have been succeeded by the tolerance of other groups and the prosperity of a disciplined life 'in the world.' John Wesley used to say to the "people called Methodists"—"make all you can, save all you can, give all you can"; but later the first two injunctions proved stronger than the, presumably, climactic third. The view of Job's friends is always triumphing over the view of Job and the writer of Job. The Protestant banker and even the Catholic banker, whose view is that of Job's friends, seem more *sensible* than the view of the *Catholic Worker* or the *Protestant Anarchist* or the Gospels. "How hardly shall a rich man enter the Kingdom of Heaven"; yet how entitled they feel to rule the world, including 'the churches,' Jonathan Edwards had occasion to discover. And "the children of this world are wiser in their generation than the children of light," as Jesus dispassionately observed.

Robinson had even less capacity for joy than Henry Adams, and, if anything, less capacity to reach any faith —religious or metaphysical. For the poor, faith in some system is some comfort. Henry Adams had an income of $50,000 a year, and despite his skepticisms could afford to keep a grand house in Washington, an apartment in Paris, and to make long trips to Japan and the South Sea islands; and he knew everyone who mattered in scholarship, politics, and art. Robinson, rescued from a menial job in the New York subway system by the intervention of that would-be Renaissance figure, Theodore Roosevelt, had for five years a job in the New York Customs House, a job without duties. When Taft became President and he was discharged from his honorary pension, he had from 1916 to 1921 an annual subsidy of $1,200 from twelve anonymous friends, rounded up by a Peterborough acquaintance.

But, endowed not with $1,200 but '50,000 a year,' Robinson would doubtless have been not so different. His friends, unlike those of Adams, were all obscure people, failures; but, like Adams, who knew them, he saw little to admire in the currently great and famous. Nor did he have any sanguine view of the age he lived in: "How the devil," he wrote a friend in 1897, "is a man to understand things in an age like this, when the whole trend of popular thought is in the wrong direction—not only that, but proud of the way it is taking? The age is all right, material progress is all right, Herbert Spencer is all right, hell is all right. These things are temporal necessities, but they are damned uninteresting to one who can get a glimpse of the real light through the clouds of time. It is that glimpse that makes me wish to live and see it out. If it were not for that glimpse, I should be tempted, as Tennyson used to be, to stick my nose in a rag soaked with chloroform and be done with it—that is, if I could screw up my courage."

Our newspaper photographers force all their subjects to smile, even those (of whom there are some) to whom a really fulsome smile is completely inapposite. I respect Robinson for not even trying. His concern is for complete honesty about himself and about the world as he sees it.

In a letter to Harry De Forest Smith, written in 1894, he says, "I must acknowledge the dismal truth that the majority of mankind interest me only as studies. . . . As you know, I seldom laugh. . . . Real solid laughter is almost a physical impossibility with me. When it occurs it almost frightens me." He praises—of Shakespeare —*Measure for Measure*, *Troilus and Cressida* (if not "the nicest play of them all, ... the widest, which is perhaps the same thing)," and lastly *Timon of Athens* ("the narrowest of the plays, . . . which is perhaps the most entertaining of them all—in a restricted sense"). His choices—and the qualifications with which they are hedged about—are first Robinsonian and then New England.

Robinson's taste in reading—as one sees from both his dedicated sonnets and his letters—took its own line: his taste for Cowper's *The Task*, for Crabbe, for Hardy, even for Zola. Among American writers, whether in verse or prose, Hawthorne alone seems to have engaged him—Hawthorne and Hawthorne's antonym, Emerson.

He had, strangely, no interest in New England history —to which he had more or less equal right with Hawthorne—an interest which gives ballast to Hawthorne and Adams and to Robert Lowell—even, in dilution, to Emerson. He seems never to have read George Gissing, who might, among the English, have been to his taste. But he had no intention of becoming a teacher or a critic or a lecturer, and seems for the most part to have read what came his way.

His early exotic taste was for the French verse forms like the villanelle: helps, doubtless, to the concision of his early poems like "Richard Cory"; in any event, practice pieces at careful, slow, meticulous writing. I can see, I think, that this fondness for villanelles and sonnets was some kind of inheritance from the long Robinson tradition of carpentry and craftsmanship, earlier practiced by his family on boat-building. In the days of Amy Lowell, some one asked him whether he wrote 'free verse' and he replied, in his customary laconic style, "No, I write badly enough as it is."

His earlier anthologized poems are too crisp in their way; his long narrative poems (written in part at least to make money for his nieces and his own hypothetic old age) are too diffuse, but both are careful in their syntax and diction. And there can be little doubt that his prolonged study of French novels and villanelles, as well as his admiring, attentive perusal of Henry James's "Lesson of the Master," was his chief training.

Amy Lowell got him into her book *Tendencies in Modern American Poetry* (1917), but she didn't get him into any 'movement.' He was too old, too isolated, had been far too many years a failure by the Yankee standards of Gardiner, Maine. The popular success of *Tristram* (1927) came too late for him to forget that success is failure and failure is success—or, in Christian language, that "He who saveth his life shall lose it, and he who loseth his life shall save it."

With his divided Yankee nature, he couldn't, of course, be regretful that he could now pay his financial debts and earn his financial living; still more, feel that Gardiner, Maine, so long ashamed of him, was now proud. "An ancient rural cousin, in the old back farm of Whitefield, saw his picture in a mail-order catalogue and yielded all his doubts." But could that gratifying recognition really alter his felt judgment that art—or some kind of contemplative activity—was higher than 'business'?

Into his 1925 volume, *Dionysus in Doubt*, Robinson gathered his sonnet on "New England"—and "conscience."

> Here where the wind is always north-north-east
> And children learn to walk on frozen toes,
> Wonder begets an envy of all those
> Who boil elsewhere with such a lyric yeast
> Of love that you will hear them at a feast
> Where demons would appeal for some repose,
> Still clamoring where the chalice overflows
> And crying wildest who have drunk the least.
> Passion is here a soilure of the wits
> We're told, and Love a cross for them to bear;
> Joy shivers in the corner where she knits
> And Conscience always has the rocking chair,
> Cheerful as when she tortured into fits
> The first cat that was ever killed by care.

According to an able critic of Robinson's, this poem was intended by the poet to caricature those young writers who prided themselves on their emancipation from Puritanism. When it was published in the Gardiner *Journal* early in 1924, and a serious subscriber wrote in protesting, Robinson wrote the editor that he had designed "an oblique attack on all those who are forever throwing dead cats [at New England] for its alleged emotional and moral frigidity."

The critic's comment and the poet's do not quite settle the matter. First, I am not aware that New England has ever been accused of "moral frigidity"—so far as I understand what that means. And the choice line, "And Conscience always has the rocking-chair"—that is, the most comfortable chair as well as the one always in motion, or capable of perpetual motion—seems to me scarcely ironic, either about New England generally or about Robinson in particular. Things are not necessarily either ironic or not ironic. But there is certainly a dash or two of irony in this sonnet, and there is a delightful fantasy in the opening lines, and there is fun in the last two lines. Does that add to 'irony'? It does add up to obliqueness.

The only other poem by a New Englander which this at all reminds me of is Thoreau's published in *A Week*. Can anyone doubt that Thoreau was one of the most conscientious not only of objectors but of affirmers? But he does attack the word and the 'indoor' and ecclesiastical connotations it then had. For this pious conscience he wanted to substitute: "A sentence should read as if its author, had he held a plow instead of a pen, could have drawn a furrow deep and straight to the end," that is, there is nothing in life which isn't a matter of conscience, and so everything secular is sacred, just as everything that is sacred can—all too easily—become secular.

Robinson's sense of conscience shares much with Thoreau's but with a difference. Both want, in a way and to a degree, to protest against the narrowing of conscience to the Anglo-Saxon, Protestant, village code. Good writing is as much a matter of conscience as good ploughing or honest shopkeeping. But Robinson *seems* —and I think was—more troubled than Thoreau: his periodic alcoholism was one symptom.

New England standards had deteriorated in the period after the Civil War, and Adams, Henry James, and Robinson could no longer live there. I see something in common between all three which is partly, but only partly, prefigured in Thoreau.

Conscience is turning into consciousness—not, of course, of oneself: the English segregation of moral consciousness from all other kinds is not giving way but transcending itself in a consciousness of which *morality* is but a part—so that the old New England conscience, admirable as in its way it was, is taking on new dimensions.

In 1915 Robinson wrote the poem which shows this consciousness—*The Man Against the Sky*—an impressive long-short philosophical poem. This is a kind of Henry Adams poem—the only one which Robinson wrote. How summarize it? How excerpt from it?

A man—Everyman—is seen at sunset time. One sees him for a moment, and then he goes down the other side of the hill. As one doesn't know him, he has all the possibilities of the anonymous man of philosophy, not the more or less determined man of fiction. He may have gone down painfully to a solitary depth. He may have gone easily, to assumed solid ground. He may have been a Stoic, or that more rigorous form of Stoic, the Cynic. He may have been a materialist or a skeptic. In any case, there is an "orient Word that will not be erased,/ Or, save in incommunicable gleams . . . Be found or known" —some Emersonian "gleam." At all events communism —or its capitalistic equivalent, "communal repose"— will not satisfy us, nor science, which says the individual matters only through the Race. Perhaps there is no solution to the human condition of "a little wisdom and much pain." Perhaps the dead die and there is no future life to compensate our pains and answer our questions.

The poem ends with the suggestion of suicide—not too difficult *if* we are nothing now and nothing after now. Yet the answer to this 'dreadful night' vision of life is not, for Robinson as a man, the suicide finally hinted. The "gleam" is enough to keep him going.

This was Robinson's great poem, published in 1916. Thereafter came the honors: the celebration of his fiftieth birthday; the *Collected Poems* (1921) selling 5,000 the first year. After 1922 there was no further need of subsidy, and by virtue largely of 'commercial accident,' *Tristram* became in 1927 his best-selling poem, his widest read. But his New England conscience found reason for a new kind of anxiety here: didn't the popular success of the poem show that Robinson's quality as a poet was deteriorating? He needed to be reassured.

After *Tristram,* each of his new narrative poems sold eight to ten thousand copies. Some critics suggested that Robinson was writing too much. But, after sixty, the "dread of destitution in his old age had returned"; no words could reassure him: "a poet who has stopped writing is just an old man, and he can't be helped." To one friend he said: "The critics are pretty severe with me nowadays. And I know, too, that I've published too frequently in the last ten years. No poet can afford to bear a new volume every year. . . . But what could I do? I needed the money. I just had to have it." Though this was no longer true, the only reassurance that could be given him was that he had never "let a careless line leave" his hands—the 'good conscience' of careful workmanship.

He died of cancer at sixty-five, writing till the end denunciations of American business and businessmen; died, too, affirming as he had all his life, that he was an idealist, not a materialist, and, least of all, a pessimist. The repeated charge—warranted, it would seem to a careful reader—that he was a pessimist appears most to have angered him. In 1932 he wrote his old friend Mrs. Richards: "Of course I am never really bitter, or anything but cheerful and full of metaphysical joy and hope; but people didn't seem to understand that and so call me all sorts of names which also they don't understand. So far as I can make out, most people are so afraid of life that when they see it coming their first impulse is to get behind a tree and shut their eyes. And for some odd reason they call that impulse optimism—which has always seemed funny to me." To an interested acquaintance he wrote, "there is no sense in saying that this world is not a pretty difficult place, but that isn't pessimism."

I have read in one of the 'critics' that Robinson's letters are 'flat.' The remark has puzzled me. They are flat only in a Yankee kind of way: matter-of-fact, blunt. In many ways they are the best introduction to the poetry, which, when it is not too short and finely sandpapered, is diffuse: kept going by what Robinson never lacked in his poetry—a rigid syntax (one kind of Yankee backbone) which reviewers variously ascribed to Browning and Henry James, neither of whom he seems much to have read. Unlike Yeats, he wrote poems and prose with different hands. But both hands wrote honestly.

To return to *pessimism* and *conscience:* Robinson didn't in the least relish American so-called optimism. He thought it the part of wisdom to be prepared for the worst; then any amelioration is relief, a bonus. Life is "a pretty difficult place": who, in his right mind, ever said it wasn't? That isn't pessimism, that is realism. Pessimism is simply the tiresome, simple, all-too-American reverse of its even more tiresome other side—optimism. The good man has no business with either illusion.

Conscience is doing one's job conscientiously—not fooling oneself or wasting one's time. For the rest, *it* is a part of consciousness: always to be attentive, alert, and, if one is a literary man, reporting what one sees when one is widest awake.

There is yet one more thing to add: Conscience requires utmost veracity with oneself and with others. This shows itself even in syntax: and *The Man Against the Sky* shows its cerebral structure in the repeated, and structurally located, conjunctions and conjunctive adverbs—the alternative possibilities of interpretation: "or," "again," "or maybe," "may have," "if," "or."

New England once had, in its intellectuals, dogmatic assurance. By the times of Adams and Robinson, such dogmatic assurance is no longer possible to the lettered. But one can keep himself from feigning an assurance he no longer feels and from uttering dogmas all too plainly subjective.

THE LAST PURITANS

In the mid-1930's were published two novels which have their proper place as public epilogues to this book —John Marquand's *The Late George Apley* (1937) and George Santayana's *The Last Puritan* (1935).

My grandparents were still living; and the early dinner, after the Boston and Albany train had deposited my grandfather at one of the Newtons, was followed by reading aloud. There being, strangely, no 'good' twentieth-century novels, the reading was generally from Dickens. But *The Late George Apley*, viewed by the young intellectuals I knew as a satire on Boston, did not so seem to my grandparents. Here, at last, was one novel about proper people written in a proper tone.

Santayana's novel did not come to their attention, and, had it done so, they would certainly have disliked it. But both books are works of art, and each, in its way, is veracious.

There is, I think, no "last Puritan," though certainly the number diminishes. And both Marquand and Santayana—half-outsiders—respect their heroes, who are Roman senators and Stoics upon whose regimen the Goths and Vandals are intruding. Apley is provincial but not ridiculous. Oliver Alden is a type of the human spirit.

Both books purport to be memoirs, undertaken at the request of another: George Apley's at the request of his son, John, who has migrated from Boston to New York; Santayana's, at the request of Oliver Alden's cousin Mario.

There the resemblance stops. Apley's memoirist is a professional Boston biographer, who would suppress all he could which might seem improper, and who gives the truth rather than the legend only at the bidding of the subject's son, who is paying for his writing the book in order that fifteen copies may be published for the immediate members of the family; Santayana writes in his own person as an ex-professor at Harvard whose best student Alden was, and writes less for the 'story' than for the 'legend'—that is, for the philosophical meaning of a life. Apley's biographer is less bright than Apley; Alden's may well be, as Alden's cousin suggests, one who 'reads into' Alden's thought his own.

(1)

Marquand's *The Late George Apley* is, to my knowledge, an accurate and affectionate as well as amusing portrait of a Bostonian who was born in 1866 and died in 1933, Harvard, class of 1887.

It is the Boston custom to have published, for the family only, some chronicle of the deceased; but Marquand enriches his novel by having Apley's son, who has migrated to New York, request, and empower, Boston's professional biographer of the upper-classed deceased, not to suppress his father's deviations from the waxen norm. The richness of the novel lies in the many points of view from which Apley is seen. The professional biographer, Apley's Harvard contemporary Mr. Willing, has a commonplace enough mind and, apart from his reluctant acquiescence in the son's wishes, shows clearly enough his own attitudes, sometimes sound but so platitudinously expressed as to make them false.

The most dramatic episode in Apley's life is the falling in love with an Irish girl from South Boston, in consequence of which misjudgment he is sent to England and the Continent with his uncle and aunt—and his cousin Henrietta, who has, with almost equal misjudgment, fallen in love with the heir of crude Pittsburgh wealth.

The biographer prints extracts from letters written to George upon his sailing, and comments: "There are no copies extant of George Apley's answers to these letters, if indeed he did answer them. For a mind as deeply disturbed as his he may quite probably have gone on the New England principle that the least said the soonest mended. He was meeting the *severe shock* which *comes to all of us who must reconcile inclination with obligation.* . . . Much of the irresponsibility which may have endeared him, but had also made him difficult, to many of his associates seems to have left him at this phase of his career."

Apley finds London very like Boston, especially when he writes his mother, "London after all is only a greater [that is, larger] Boston . . . It is only that there is more of everything. There are more Louisburg Squares, more Beacon Streets, and more Clubs. . . ." The Champs Elysées is surprisingly like Commonwealth Avenue.

His biographer, Willing, quotes from his European notebooks "one excerpt which may seem both unusual and disturbing:

" 'As I stood on the edge of this village and looked up the white road winding between its hedges through that rolling farm country, I wished that I might be walking up it to see something by myself and for myself without guidance and without advice. I wonder, will I ever walk up any road alone.' "

George returns to Boston. He is tried out, tested, for his business ability by his Uncle William, owner of the cotton mills at Apley Falls. He fails, two successive summers, and in consequence his father wills him an inheritance *under trust*, after a mode increasingly true with such Boston families. The fathers, who made the money, mistrust their sons' ability to carry on the business—deem them not shrewd enough or hard enough. George's biographer wishes to deny the accusation that this system has "atrophied the abilities" of the *epigones*, and observes, "Relieved of the burden of caring for a large financial estate our leading citizens have never shirked their duty to the community"—which is quite Uncle William's view: "I am very sure that George would be a successful guardian of other people's money, but not of his own."

George's marriage is arranged for him—to one of his own class, Catherine Bosworth. It is not a romantic marriage, and Catherine is the more dominant of the couple. The references to Catherine in George's letters to his friends and to his son and daughter are always tactful, but the implication is of an inflexibility beyond George's. But in those days divorce was rare; and, as Biographer Willing, more wisely than he knows, observes: "Those concessions so necessary in the bond of matrimony were more readily arranged because, in a sense, they were inevitable."

Having graduated from Harvard Law School, Apley has a place found for him with a legal firm already known for its management of real estate and searching of titles. The latter pursuit, carried on in the Registry of Deeds, suggested to him the history of a North End business corner in which his firm is interested, and he traces the successive owners of the property back to the seventeenth century, when Jonas Good owned it, and forward to its present owner, Luigi Martinelli, restaurateur. He has not only traced the 115 owners of 'Cow Corner,' but even located the graves where fifty-six of them are buried. This antiquarian study he reads before the Browsers' Club, to which he has recently been elected; and, says his biographer, "thus almost overnight he took his place with the intellectual element of the city." It is read and commended, even by President Eliot of Harvard, and (privately published a week later) leads to Apley's being invited to join the Historical Society, the Colonial Society, and many others. Nearly every evening, Catherine and he dine out, listening thereafter to a 'paper'; and frequently there follows a later evening party, "with music and another paper read and a supper of creamed oysters." Meanwhile, his afternoons are given over to the board meetings of charitable organizations.

So, like many Americans, including women, he leads an 'active' life, yet is unsatisfied. He says to his biographer, "I seem to be busy all the time but I don't seem to be doing anything."

He needs cruises and periods in the woods. Finally, he takes a bold step. Finding Pequod Island, in one of Maine's lakes, he decides to buy the island and make it a haven for men. But after two years, his wife and sister beg to be included in the party; in consequence of which Apley has to organize a group within a group, the "camping crowd," made up always of men, provided with canoes and cabins. And neither his wife nor his sister can interfere with the "camping crowd" and its activities.

In 1905, the year when his portrait is painted by J. S. Sargent, he first becomes aware that "his caste in a sense was threatened." He writes his sister, "We must and we shall clean up Boston. If we do not, this will become an Irish city run by the Roman Catholic Church," and he is one of the early organizers of the Save Boston Association, intended to stimulate the public conscience to the corruption in city government. His Uncle William warns him that he is undertaking something beyond his experience. Apley replies to his uncle, "I neither like nor enjoy what I am doing. . . . you may be right in what you say . . . , but I feel this to be my duty. I am sorry I must go ahead."

George's son John, a Groton man, distinctly of the next generation, sees his father clearly. George writes his son a father's proper letters: "I am very sorry that you are unhappy and sometime soon I am coming up to see you, but you must remember that no one can be happy all the time. I believe that a large part of life consists of learning how to be unhappy without worrying too much about it. . . ." And he complains of his son's low grades.

But John understands, even as a boy. "I could understand," he writes Biographer Willing, "that Father had a great many worries, not the sort that would worry most people, but genuine, none the less." There were "the details in his life, which he was working at conscientiously. He was getting himself involved in an infernal round of detail. . . . All these matters were assuming for him a peculiar and completely overestimated importance, so characteristically Bostonian. He was always doing a hundred things, not one of them amounting to much, and it was like him never to let anything go when he might have dropped the whole lot of them without any trouble. I never blamed him when he was hard on me because he *was hard on himself—too hard.*"

There is no 'moral' to Marquand's book, though plenty of morals. Apley realizes himself to be an *epigone* —not comparable in boldness to his father and his grandfather. "I have always been faced from childhood by the obligation of convention, and all of these conventions have been made by others. . . . In some way these have stepped in between me and life. . . . They were designed to promote stability and inheritance. Perhaps they have gone a bit too far."

What are the things he has really cared about most? Generally, simple things. They have been the relaxation after physical weariness—the feel of wind on the face, the feel of cold water on the body or being "near the woods or water at sundown." "All this has been very good. Yet somehow I seem to have enjoyed few of these pleasures, for I have never seemed to have time to enjoy them. . . . I have sometimes deliberately tried not to enjoy them. I have turned away from them because I have believed that most of these were pleasures of the senses rather than of the intellect."

That is one boundary of Apley's oscillation. The other soon follows. "There is a great deal of talk in these days about happiness.... Perhaps it would be better if people realized that happiness comes only by indirection, that it can never exist by any conscious effort of the will."

Apley isn't sure—too sure—of himself. None of his 'reflections' can be quoted as representing a steady view: *that*, shall we say, endears him. He is not a *grim* Puritan. Sometimes he feels that his *environment* has thwarted him; at other times that no other environment could both have suited him and found a place for him. As meant, all these 'reflections' are true. But when I think of him as one of the 'last Puritans,' I think mostly of his conscientiousness. He is, as the directions for his own funeral show as well as anything, faithful to his way of life, in detail. That, indeed, is, I think, what we mean by 'conscientiousness'—to me a somewhat ambivalent term. Conscience may give one melodramatic moments of decision; conscientiousness faithfully pursues the little things, the 'hundreds of details.' Implicit in conscientiousness are doubtless principles, such as order, hierarchy, loyalty; but the conscientious man doesn't need—in fact, rather shrinks from—religious or philosophical doctrines which more or less overtly call attention to this incarnational quality of routine regularly and faithfully performed.

One kind of 'last Puritan' is the preserver of traditional ways, the conscientious man, the man of detail and order, who seeks to transmit, unimpaired, what he has received. The first Puritans were Reformers; the last Puritan may be a curator.

(2)

Santayana's one novel, *The Last Puritan,* is an *Erziehungsroman.*

Why, in Part I, Ancestry, the author represents his fictitious Peter Alden, father of the 'hero,' as son of the historic hard landlord and miser, Dr. Parkman, murdered by Professor Webster of Harvard, I can only guess; and I could give many plausible guesses—historical, Freudian, Christian. Let me loosely say that exacting what is due you is a Puritan duty, and bookkeeping is likewise a Puritan duty, and that public gifts to public charities can never take the place of Catholic or secular spontaneous warmheartedness.

Then, at Harvard, a secret society with initiation rites commands Peter to break into the Chapel one night and purloin the Bible from its hallowed place on the reading ledge of the high pulpit. The consequence is that a nightwatchman is killed—in part, because the Sacred Book fell upon him. Here seems more room for symbolic guessing.

It is thought best for Peter to leave the college and the country. He takes his M.D. abroad, but never practices; wanders around the world in his yacht; temporarily becomes a patient of the leading American psychiatrist, Dr. Bumstead, of Great Falls, Connecticut; at forty, interrupts his travels long enough to marry Bumstead's daughter, Harriet, and beget a son.

The only offspring, Oliver, is born a philosopher. "There were good things and there were bad things, and there was an equal duty to pull through both." Since his mother dislikes children, he has a German governess, richly endowed with quotations from Goethe but also simply affectionate; yet "he would not have been bored running about silently by himself." Before he is five, he begins lessons, lessons given him in his high chair. Never "did it cross Oliver's dutiful mind to fret or break off. Life was essentially something to be endured, something grim. There was no reasonableness in rebelling simply because for the moment things might be unpleasant."

At fifteen, Oliver is sent to the Great Falls High School. He is best at sports; best at his studies; but he has—if no foes—no friends. "All his lessons and sports seemed to be taken up as duties and executed unswervingly, as if to get rid of them as quickly and thoroughly as possible." He shows at school "the same docility, the same pluck, and the same sadness with which he had done his lessons at home, and taken his exercise." Mrs. Alden and Fraulein Irma both perceive this joylessness. Says Irma, "Oliver needs more friends, more sympathy, and yet the friends he makes and all their attentions seem to mean little to him, *except more weight of obligation.*"

Permitted, Irma writes Dr. Alden, who bids Oliver join him on his yacht, "The Black Swan," anchored in Boston Harbor. Here he meets a young Englishman called 'Lord Jim' after the flawed hero of Conrad's story. 'Lord Jim' is Oliver's first experience at friendship and hero worship. But 'Lord Jim' has much to teach him—first of all, about Dr. Alden, of whose guilt-inducing accident in the Harvard Chapel Oliver had never heard, and whose free use of drugs shocks Oliver even more. And next something about Jim's naval career and its ending. Next summer, Oliver joins his father and 'Lord Jim' in England and learns Jim's 'domestic' secrets. 'Lord Jim' takes him to an inn: the married landlady is his mistress, and 'Lord Jim' has a son by her. And then comes the story of Jim's father, a Christian Platonist and a gentleman who, reading for holy orders at Oxford, met by chance once, and then again occasionally, a farmer's daughter. "The wedding had to be hastened, and poor Pater had to confess everything to his superiors and got a bad name for life, and a wife that other clergymen's ladies wouldn't visit."

This series of disillusionments is perhaps all that need be narrated of the novel's 'story.' Not too long after, Oliver's father takes just the right overdose of sleeping pills and wakes up no more. And his mother, who appears (as is intended) too late to prevent *it*, is the "self-assertive woman" with whose fables, fancies, and whims Oliver is patiently courteous.

There are, however, a few people who understand Oliver—the first, Jim's father, the vicar of the old church at Iffley—a saint despite his early lapse. He is a kind of Christian Platonist whose views of Christianity are not too unlike those which Santayana expressed in his early books on religion. To Oliver, at their first meeting, he says, "You, my friend, if I am not mistaken, are an ἀνήρ πνευματικός, a spiritual man by nature: I am not not sure how far, without loss of anything better, you might be an athlete or a soldier or a lover of women." And there is his father who, shortly before he dies, thinks to himself, "Certainly this boy is atavistic. He has skipped his parents and drawn his character from his remote ancestors. He's like a two-edged sword, as merciless in one direction as in the other."

But, most of all, there is Oliver himself. "The old Calvinists, Oliver felt, hadn't been puritan enough: you were not pure at all, unless it was for the love of purity: but with them *it* had been a mean calculation of superstition and thrift and vengeance—vengeance against everybody who was happier and better than themselves." Perhaps, Oliver's thinking goes on, there is no single moral standard—certainly not the historic Puritan's invocation of "their hard, dry reason to discredit all that was beyond their own meagre and cruel morality." He invokes the modes he knows, including his own: "... burdened but strong, groping but faithful, desolate but proud." "It was a foolish debate: free and infinite spirit ... could never stop short at any point and say: This is truly right, this is perfect, this is supreme."

How, then, can a spiritual man who is by nature a puritan strive to make all other men puritans; to reform them, to persecute them if their center is not his? Purity is its own reward—yes, and its own deprivation.

Can there be an "austerity" (the word Santayana several times uses of Oliver in his last years) which rejects the world, the flesh, and the devil, which rejects the sensuous and the sensual, the pleasures of the *gourmet* and the libertine, even the pleasures of literature and the mythology and ritual of religion, and yet holds no contempt for those who need them, enjoy them, use them?

Not often, probably; rarely, probably. Yet such an ideal can be adumbrated. Such a man can see the world—and other men—as they are, without bitterness or without the desire to convert—still less, to persecute—them. He can be drawn to types unlike his own and acquire some understanding of them: his nature is honest, just, but cold; and they warm him and teach him. But he is not really capable of love. He wants to know. The good others do him is to give him, by observation and as near as he can reach to empathy—what love, as the ordinary man comprehends it, is like.

Santayana endows Oliver with wealth, with health, with good looks—the attributes which might draw him to the world as the world to him. He is the rich young ruler of Jesus' parable.

The 'moral virtues' are equally his. He is even, without naming it, an ascetic. He has a repulsion at the idea of drugs ("dope"); he dislikes not only whiskey but beer, prefers milk; likes a hard bed. He never cared much, even in childhood, for tales and stories and jokes. The "puritan disdain of human weakness and of human genius" was already at work within him.

He is scrupulously considerate of others—in his life, in his gifts, in his 'last will and testament.' But he cannot, either temporarily or permanently, give himself—for himself is his conscience, his principles.

Yet this justice is only one aspect of his deep sense of responsibility. *Noblesse oblige* is a fine, aristocratic maxim. With Oliver, American and ostensible democrat as he is, the more wealth he has, the more of everything he has, the more enslaved he is. He can't, with a magnificent gesture, strip himself of it all; he has too many *responsibilities.* Money may give pleasure to some; to him it is like his athletic ability, a solemn trust.

In some earlier period he could have become a Catholic monk. In the twentieth century, Santayana thinks, he might have become a communist (surely of the purest, the Trotskyite, variety). What he clearly likes, so far as he can be said to like anything, is voluntarily to subject himself to some rule. But the submission must be voluntary and to some cause, some set of principles, of which he approves.

The historical Puritans knew what it was to sin and to repent, to love falsely and to love truly. Man is a fallen creature: he has to come, emotionally and cognitively, to recognition and confession of his state before he can love other creatures and the Creator. Oliver, the 'last,' because the theoretical, Puritan, is sinless and hence incapable of love; he is purely a contemplative. Life is sad if one is caught in its network, its reticulation, of sin and loving; how much sadder if one can't be so caught—if the caughtness of others is the cause only of shock and of alienness? Then the 'last Puritan' becomes purified out of the world of existence and has, like Oliver, to be killed off early, by accident, for he is not existentially real: he is but a noble abstraction—a graph on a conceptual blackboard.

AN APPENDED NOTE

Conscience and Toleration

It is easy to be tolerant of others in matters which do not centrally concern us—that is, tolerant in matters to which we are indifferent.

A favorite formula of the seventeenth-century divines was to distinguish between fundamental matters, in which agreement should be required or disagreement not permitted, and issues not fundamental, in which differences might be tolerated. But this maxim, which sounds so sensible, is not so easy to apply. To take an instance from disputes in the Anglican Church, does it matter whether the minister wear a black Geneva gown, a white surplice, a white chasuble, or a colored chasuble? One might say that these are all matters of externals or ritual; but most people feel—and rightly—that ritual is the outer expression of an inner attitude; it implies—except in the instance of the sheerest ecclesiastical milliners—a doctrine concerning the Lord's Supper, the Communion, the Eucharist, the

Mass—just as the choice of terms for the service itself are not mere variants of nomenclature.

Probably religion, politics, sexual morality, war are matters which concern all men. There are, to be sure, 'conscientious objectors' to war; but then there are, I am sure, conscientious atheists, communists, anarchists, nudists, polygamists, free lovers; and there are conscientious vegetarians. It seems easier for a lawyer or a government to recognize this 'conscientiousness' when it is the tenet and practice of a recognized and—so to speak—established religion; in these cases, it becomes a matter of a small group being loyal to its principles though they bring it into conflict with the principles, even the civil laws, of a far larger group—the nation. But this distinction seems a mere convenience. Any individual who, according to his lights, has thought through an issue and emerged with a view contrary to that of his neighbors can scarcely be denied the epithet 'conscientious'—even though, as John Jay Chapman says of William Lloyd Garrison, it is "his local, momentary conscience," which may change next year, or tomorrow

In a stable, or relatively stable, society, a considerable amount of conscientious objection can be tolerated without real danger of political, social, or psychological anarchy. England has long been rich in eccentrics; and the New England village of my youth could manage a considerable number. I speak of eccentrics, because external deviations from the norm of human behavior may—as with Thoreau and Emily Dickinson—constitute something like the external armor of village folk whose inner life has a public worth probably not possible without the armor.

Eccentric individuals are, on the whole, so far as I can judge, tolerant of those from whose norms they deviate: they "accept the universe." A really difficult matter is the tolerance by a tolerating society of organized groups, whether communist or New England Puritan or Roman Catholic, which claim toleration when they are in a minority but which, when in power, do not tolerate in turn. Such groups consider themselves to be in possession of the Truth; and to tolerate other claimants would be to tolerate heresy or—to use a politer modern term—error. Liberals of all sorts, whether ecclesiastical, political, or other, are here caught in an embarrassing situation, for they do not lay claim to infallibility or even to the whole truth. Their plea is, indeed, for an open arena in which all approximate truths and half-truths may be honestly represented, may contend with one another. Their firmest conviction is that of Milton, in his *Areopagitica,* that freedom from partisanship, sectarianism, and censorship is the negative condition under which, alone, men can arrive at an approximation to absolute truth.

Toleration as a principle is, when pushed to its positive consequence, the view that one not only should not coerce others (by political or corporal punishment) to adopt—or profess to adopt—one's views, but that one should not even argue one's own views too powerfully against an unequal opponent—unequal in learning, in intellectual or dialectical power—for there is a kind of authority which even learning and reasoning can exert; and in "fundamental matters" it seems that every man must hear both sides argued by minds of equal power and skill —even more, that in "fundamental matters" the total self should be reached and converted or confirmed. Rhetoric reaches the emotions: logical argument, the intellect; neither is adequate for that slow, mature process by which we reach life convictions—what, combining two central words from Newman's works and thought, I may call illative assent.

The unfortunate thing about both the word and the concept, toleration, seems the negative tone. Toleration, it appears, is the lesser of two evils; or, in even more vulgar form, it means that I tolerate you and your beliefs, absurd or crude as they are, as a condition to your tolerating mine. Missing is the concept that out of a give and take, a dialectic which is not merely carried on in the mind of one philosopher, something more comprehensively true may emerge; missing is the concept, more vague and more difficult to place existentially, that "Great is truth and will prevail." To 'tolerate' is to endure something. Can I not believe that, spoken out of honesty and with love, the many voices can produce something symphonic?

I feel to the full, I think, all the difficulties of this position. It seems fantastically and Utopianly democratic. Surely there are, in a generation, only a few persons so endowed and so trained as to be able to think—or, as Professor Stebbins with unconscious pomposity calls it, to "think to some purpose." And what are the philosophers of one generation when compared with Aristotle and his great teacher, Plato, of whose writings Whitehead not extravagantly said, "The whole history of philosophy is but a series of footnotes" to them?

But what we are called upon to 'tolerate'—that is, the *Weltanschauung* of others—is not professional philosophy. The aristocratically minded Santayana does something like justice in his essay on William James, who did more than just tolerate Benjamin Paul Blood and his *Anaesthetic Revelations* and Anne Payson Call's *Power through Repose.* Until the last curtain was rung down, Santayana writes, James wished "the intellectual cripples and the moral hunchbacks not to be jeered at; perhaps they might turn out to be the heroes of the play. Who could tell what heavenly influences might not pierce to these sensitive half-flayed creatures, which are lost on the thick-skinned, the sane, and the duly goggled?"

NOTES

Chiefly Bibliographical

CONSCIENCE AND ITS PATHOLOGY

Highly useful for my purposes are the historical accounts, ethnically arranged, of "Babylonian," "Egyptian," "Greek and Roman," "Jewish," and "Muslim" thought in Hastings' *Encyclopaedia of Religion and Ethics* (1911), and so, too, is the sociological account in Edward Westermarck's *Origin and Development of the Moral Ideas* (1912), I, 131 ff., "Analysis of the Principal Moral Concepts."

The standard Roman Catholic treatment, topically arranged, is to be found in the *Dictionnaire de théologie catholique*, ed. A. Vacant, *et al.* (1909–50). This French Encyclopaedia, under 'Conscience,' gives its subtopics as: 1. La conscience psychologique. 2. La conscience morale. 3. Raison d'être de la conscience morale. 4. Éléments intellectuels de la conscience morale. 5. Analyse de l'acte de conscience. 6. Éléments affectifs de la conscience morale. 7. Origines de la conscience morale. 8. Propriétés de la conscience morale. 9. Fausses prétentions de la conscience. 10. *Les maladies de la conscience.*

There are useful treatments of conscience in J. H. Muirhead's *Elements of Ethics* (1892), James Martineau's *Types of Ethical Theory* (3d ed., revised; 1898—especially "Incidental Tests of the Theory of Conscience," II, 54 ff.), and F. H. Bradley's *Ethical Studies* (2d ed.; 1927).

Casuistry has, as a word, fallen into disrepute, but its referent, problems of conscience—the difficulty of knowing which general ethical law to apply in a particular case (especially when such general laws seem to conflict)—was never more important. The 'literature' (Jewish, Roman Catholic, Anglican, Puritan) is vast. The English classic is doubtless Bishop Jeremy Taylor's *Ductor Dubitantium* (1660), of which Hawthorne says that, "full of cases of conscience," it is a book "in which most men possessed of a conscience may find something applicable to their purpose." The most bold and useful to me have been the books of Bishop Kenneth Kirk, *The Threshold of Ethics* (1933) and *Conscience and Its Problems: an Introduction to Casuistry* (1927).

Casuistry is not only a systematic subject for theory. In practice it takes the form of 'spiritual letters'; and here I would recommend above all those of Fénelon, archbishop of Cambrai (1651–1715) and Baron Friedrich von Hügel (1852–1925).

Henri Bremond's *Histoire littéraire du sentiment religieux en France . . .*, Vol. I, *L'Humanisme dévot* (1916) and Msgr. Ronald Knox's *Enthusiasm: a Chapter in the History of Religion* (1950) have been my steady guides, assurances, inspirations.

1. Knox, *Enthusiasm*, 211.

2. *The Literary Remains of the Late Henry James*, ed. William James (1884), pp. 293–94.

3. Benjamin Whichcote, D.D., *Moral and Religious Aphorisms*, with an Introduction by W. R. Inge, D.D., Dean of St. Paul's (1930), p. 121 (Aphorism 1058).

4. I quote here the ending of the Anglican 'General Confession,' a not very satisfactory attempt to combine Catholic and Calvinist views: the Catholic opening, the avowal that we have "left undone those things which we ought to have done," etc., is a curious effort to reconcile the specificity of the confessional

with a vagueness which one can scarcely call even Protestant: a polite vagueness.

5. W. Windelband, *History of Philosophy* ... (tr. James H. Tufts, 1893), pp. 552–54.

6. F. von Hügel, *Letters to a Niece* (1950), p. xxiii.

7. Mrs. Stowe, *The Minister's Wooing* (1859), p. 122. Much to be recommended is Charles H. Foster's *The Rungless Ladder. Harriet Beecher Stowe and New England Puritanism* (1954).

8. James Martineau, *Types of Ethical Theory*, ii, 54–64.

9. Emerson, "Lecture on the Times" (1841).

10. Fénelon, *Letters to Men* (tr. Lear), pp. 47, 51, 65.

11. Fr. J. P. de Caussade, S.J., *Abandonment, or Absolute Surrender to Divine Providence* ... (tr. McMahon, 1887), p. 6.

12. Mrs. Stowe, in her New England novels, *Oldtown Folks* and *The Minister's Wooing*, is my authority for the women; the witty remark of Samuel Eliot Morison's about the men comes from his *Builders of the Bay Colony* (1930), p. 166.

THE FIRST GOVERNORS

Strangely, no biography of Bradford was published between Cotton Mather's in the *Magnalia* (1702; reprinted, 1852) and Bradford Smith's *Bradford of Plymouth* (1951), a book praised by Samuel Eliot Morison but difficult to use, for, though it ends with a substantial bibliography and purports not to be historical fiction, it abounds in novelistic devices.

Though he supplements it by "oral tradition" or whatever, Cotton Mather did have before him, as he wrote, Bradford's history *Of Plymouth Plantation.* There is now an excellent edition of this history, with introduction and really useful notes by S. E. Morison, published in 1952. The history, however, needs supplementation, and that is well offered by George F. Willison's *Saints and Strangers* ... (1945).

Winthrop's Journal, 1630–1649 I have used in the edition of James K. Hosmer (1908), but I am greatly indebted to Edmund S. Morgan's *The Puritan Dilemma: The Story of John Winthrop* (1958), a scholarly and interpretative monograph which is a model in kind. The passages from Winthrop's letter to his wife Margaret I have excerpted from Elizabeth Hanscom's *The Heart of the Puritan: Selections from Letters and Journals* (1917).

1. The Pilgrims, as we now call them, had no name for their left-wing Puritan group. By their critics they were often called Brownists, after the name of Robert Browne, who organized such a Separatist group but later returned to the Anglican Church.

In Chapter 7, Book I, Bradford, speaking of the departure of the future Colonists from Leyden writes of them, deftly interweaving phrases from Hebrews 11:1–16, that "they knew they were pilgrims" and lifted up their eyes to "the heavens, their dearest country"; and from this passage, the Plymouth Colonists eventually—after their time—derived their name.

2. As late as the early nineteeth century, only the Episcopalians celebrated Christmas and Easter. In Mrs. Stowe's *Poganuc People,* written in 1876 in large measure out of her recollection of Litchfield, Connecticut, the Congregational clergyman, drawn from her father, gives a learned sermon denouncing Christmas as unhistoric as well as leading the way back to Anglican and Popish abuses.

3. Bradford's own handling of newcomers who wanted to play on Christmas he calls, in the right tone, a matter "rather of mirth than of weight."

4. The larger Puritan churches, like the First Church of Boston, had two clergymen, one of whom was called the "teacher" and the other the "pastor." Of the Boston church, Cotton was teacher; Wilson, pastor. As the term implies, the teacher was the theological expert and expounder, but both preached, and the differentiation of functions, never very sharp, soon disappeared.

5. Jonathan Edwards, in his sermon "A Divine and Supernatural Light," preached in 1733, clearly states the doctrine which rules out Mrs. Hutchinson and the Quakers:

"This spiritual light is not the suggesting of any new truths or propositions not contained in the Word of God [i.e., the Bible]. This suggesting of new truths or doctrines to the mind, independent of any antecedent revelation of those propositions, either in word or writing is inspiration,—such as the prophets and apostles had and such as some *enthusiasts* pretend to." The proper spiritual light "teaches no new thing of God or Christ or another world not taught in the Bible but only gives a *due apprehension* of those things that are taught in the Word of God."

ROGER WILLIAMS

As Thomas Johnson wrote in 1948 (*LHUS*, III, 774), "Williams is one of the very few colonial authors whose works have been collected. *The Writings of Roger Williams*, (1866–74), 6 vols., published by the Narragansett Club, reprints most of the letters and separate works." The pamphlets Cotton wrote in his controversy with Williams, e.g., *The Controversy Concerning Liberty of Conscience in Matters of Religion* (1646) and *The Bloody Tenent Washed and Made White in the Blood of the Lamb* (1647), are most readily accessible in the collected works of his exiled opponent—a strange, so far as I know, unique, circumstance, though we have sentences of heretics preserved only in the books of the orthodox who replied to them, after the old manner (still to be seen in Hooker's *Ecclesiastical Polity*) of point by point reply.

Perry Miller (*Roger Williams: His Contribution to the American Tradition* [1953]) has convinced me that most twentieth-century writing on Williams, hailing him as the founder of "modern secular liberalism," is not a true view of this great, strange, odd, lovable man. As Williams was orally persuasive and—in his writing—by fits and starts really eloquent, Miller has written a book which combines anthology with commentary, yet never confounding the two—a feat indeed.

Cotton was known both in England and New England as a great preacher, yet the life has gone out of his books, if, indeed, it was once in them. Perhaps more serious is one's feeling that he equivocated, let Anne Hutchinson down when he saw that she must go, played it safe. His case is a difficult one to judge. I would suppose that he had mystical *tendencies*, but grew alarmed when (under pressure) his devoted parishioner professed revelations made to her—not mere deeper openings of the Word. And he was also aware of the danger of such a doctrine in a recently established community.

Happily, there is now a recent and good monograph on him, Larzer Ziff's *The Career of John Cotton: Puritanism and the American Experience* (1962).

MICHAEL WIGGLESWORTH

My chapter is based on "The Diary of Michael Wigglesworth," published in the *Publications of the Colonial Society of Massachusetts,* XXXV (1951), 322–444. The "Diary" is edited by Edmund S. Morgan, who prefaces it with an introductory essay (*ibid.*, pp. 311–20) on "The Puritanism of Wigglesworth," from which I quote: "If worrying would have saved New England, Wigglesworth would have saved it." "If we measure him [Wigglesworth] by the precepts of the Puritan preachers, it will be apparent, I think, that his sense of guilt, his hostility to pleasure, even his minding of other people's business, were not the anomalies of a diseased mind but simply the qualities demanded of a good Puritan."

A competent and sensible recent biography of Wigglesworth is Richard Crowder's *No Featherbed to Heaven . . .* (1962).

COTTON MATHER

The *Diary* of Cotton Mather, edited by Worthington C. Ford, was first published in the *Collections of the Massachusetts Historical Society,* 7th series, vols. VII–VIII (1911–12); but, as Ford prefatorily says, the existence of the *Diary,* scattered between three libraries, had long been known. Professor Barrett Wendell made use of it in his excellent *Cotton Mather, Puritan Priest* (1891); and, indeed, as far back as 1844, William B. O. Peabody made "much use of it" (his own words, borne out by his practice) in the *Life of Cotton Mather* which he wrote for vol. VI of "The Library of American Biography," a series edited by Jared Sparks, *inter alia* professor of history and subsequently president of Harvard.

Concurrently with writing this chapter on the *Diary,* a psychological study, I wrote a longer essay on Mather's longest —and, I think, greatest book—the *Magnalia,* a basic book for historians of New England and one of the last masterpieces of Baroque prose: this will be found in the *Sewanee Review* LXXII (1964), 96–116, under the title "Grandfather Mather and His Wonder Book."

JONATHAN EDWARDS

The Yale University Press is now issuing, volume by volume, a really adequate edition of Edwards' *Works,* thus (even more appropriately than by naming one of its Colleges after him) paying recognition to its distinguished alumnus. The standard old edition is the *Works* in ten volumes edited by Edwards' grandson, Sereno E. Dwight (1829–30); the first volume is given to Edwards' *Life* written by Dwight.

Edwards' disciple, Samuel Hopkins of Newport, published a brief *Life and Character of the Late Reverend Mr. Jonathan Edwards* (1765). The fullest and best twentieth-century life is by Ola Winslow (1940); and I take this occasion to recommend also Miss Winslow's *Meetinghouse Hill, 1630–1783* (1952), a "rich" book on the New England parish church based largely on clergymen's diaries and on church records.

Perry Miller, who has done more, directly and indirectly, for the study of New England thought than any other man, published in 1949 a book on Jonathan Edwards ("American Men of Letters Series"). It is an eloquent, dramatic, and brilliant book. My reserves about it come where I shouldn't expect them to come: in his exposition of Edwards' thought—which, it seems to me, Miller translates into what (had Edwards not been hampered by an inadequate philosophical language and by writing as a theologian) he would have thought—i.e., what Miller thought. With a provincial man of genius like Edwards, the feeling that he ought to be translated is a particular temptation.

I shall end this note by a few unrandom if not closely related comments. The best volume of selections is that by Clarence Faust and Thomas Johnson ("American Writers Series," 1935). Worth close reading is the short treatise, *The Nature of True Virtue,* not published till after Edwards' death and now to be had in an Ann Arbor Paperback (1960). Robert Lowell has two finely empathic poems on Edwards in his *Lord Weary's Castle* (1946) and a third has appeared in *For The Union Dead* (1964).

Edwards is buried at Princeton (then the College of New Jersey), where he died five months after having become its president. Northampton, from the pulpit of which he was expelled in middle life, now has an Edwards Memorial Church (in nineteenth-century brownstone Gothic) as well as the First Church, which he served as pastor.

HENRY DAVID THOREAU

1. The books on Thoreau abound. I have chiefly used Joseph Wood Krutch's *Thoreau* (1948) and Sherman Paul's finely sensitive and perceptive *The Shores of America: Thoreau's Inward Exploration* (1958).

2. Thoreau's poems, of which the one I quote was first published in *A Week*, have now been assembled and edited by Carl Bode, *Collected Poems of Henry Thoreau* (1943).

3. I value highly, and use here in paraphrase, F. H. Bradley's *Ethical Studies* (1876; republished 1927), and in particular Essay v, "My Station and Its Duties." The word "station" is likely to repel or confuse the American reader; actually, Bradley seems to mean nothing more snobbish than the mathematical point which locates the "me."

4. Arnold's once famous judgment of Emerson appeared at the end of his lecture on R.W.E., published in *Discourses in America:* R.W.E.'s judgment of his own vocation will be found in Charles J. Woodbury's *Talks with Emerson* (1890), a book which remarkably apprehends the spirit of Emerson.

5. Etzler's book (written in English by a native of Germany) was the subject of an essay Thoreau published in the *Democratic Review,* VII (1843), 451–63.

6. Emerson's report first appeared in the third volume of the *Dial,* that famous transcendentalist quarterly; for Lowell, see the early pages of his essay, "Thoreau" (*My Study Windows,* 1871).

7. The brief quotation is from Gilbert Barnes's *Antislavery Impulse*... (1933).

8. Roger Burlingame, *The American Conscience* (1957), thinks of the things (slavery, denial of the vote to women, etc.) which Americans have gradually come to feel as unjust. It was, I think one might say, the "British conscience" which led the British to surrender their Indian empire: imperialism and colonialism came to seem unjust.

Burlingame is writing (though historically and not hortatorily) in the tradition of the New England Reformers—those who took up causes. He is also—in a fashion which I believe to be relatively recent—thinking of conscience not as something individual but of what might be—and indeed I believe is—called 'social conscience,' the pooled consciences of, if not a majority, at least a substantial minority, of a whole population.

9. Excellent, for perspective, and bibliography, is George Woodcock's *Anarchism: A History of Libertarian Ideas and Movements* (1962).

10. Compare the account of Brown in Bruce Catton's *This Hallowed Ground* (1955).

11. Dr. Samuel Hopkins, disciple and biographer of Jonathan Edwards, is the titular hero of Mrs. Stowe's *The Minister's Wooing* (1859), and chapters 9 and 10 vividly present the theologian's split with the wealthy slave-trading deacon of his, the Second Church of Newport.

WILLIAM LLOYD GARRISON

My interest in Garrison was aroused by John Jay Chapman's book on him, first published in 1913 and now most accessible in Chapman's *Selected Writings*, edited with an Introduction by Jacques Barzun (1957). Barzun also includes Chapman's other "polar figure," Emerson: the small book on whom appeared in 1898.

Both are brilliant, but the "Garrison" is also irritating—or at least baffling—for their author had a grandmother, Maria Weston Chapman, who was Garrison's female cohort (possessed of beauty, courage, and many other virtues) and who knew —and judged—all the ins and outs of the Antislavery cause: Chapman has a vivid portrait of her in his *Memories and Milestones* (1915), a title which gives no notion of the delights of this, probably his best book, unless it be M. A. DeWolfe Howe's *Chapman and His Letters* (1937).

But Chapman, without stopping to think, supposes that we all know the facts of Garrison's campaign and all he need do is interpret it—if that be not too solemn a word. We don't, however, and I have read the four volumes, utterly humorless and indiscriminate, by Wendell P. and Francis J. Garrison, *Garrison:*

The Story of His Life Told by His Children (1885–89)—as well as Lawrence Ladu's *The Bold Brahmins: New England's War Against Slavery 1831–1863* (1961) and Gilbert Barnes's *The Anti-Slavery Impulse, 1830–44* (1933).

1. Blaine had said, "California is capable of maintaining a vast population of Anglo-Saxon freemen if we do not surrender it to Chinese coolies."

NATHANIEL HAWTHORNE

For the view that Hawthorne was a Calvinist by intuition, cf. Herbert W. Schneider, *The Puritan Mind* (1930, now in print as an Ann Arbor Paperback), pp. 256–64, and Austin Warren, *Nathaniel Hawthorne*... ("American Writers Series," 1934), pp. XIX–XLVII. Henry James argues his case for a purely aesthetic view of Hawthorne's writing in his monograph published in the "English Men of Letters" series in 1879 and conveniently available in *The Shock of Recognition* . . . , edited by Edmund Wilson (1952).

1. Cf. A. Warren, "Hawthorne's Reading," *New England Quarterly*, VIII (1935), 480–97.

2. Melville and Hawthorne were neighbors at Lenox in 1850–51, and the former's high estimate of the latter can still be read in Melville's review of *Mosses from an Old Manse*, first published in Duyckinck's *Literary World* and conveniently available in Edmund Wilson's *Shock of Recognition*... (1952), pp. 187–204. Melville writes: "Whether Hawthorne has simply availed himself of this mystical blackness as a means to the wondrous effects he makes it produce in his lights and shades [the *chiaroscuro* of James]; or whether there really lurks in him, perhaps unknown to himself, a touch of Puritan gloom, —this, I cannot altogether tell. Certain it is, however, that this great power of blackness in him derives its force from its appeals to that Calvinistic sense of Innate Depravity and Original Sin, from whose visitations, in some shape or other, no deeply thinking mind is always and wholly free."

The two men next met when Hawthorne was consul at Liverpool and Melville on his way to the Holy Land. Hawthorne's entry, in his *English Notebooks*, has often been quoted, e.g., by Randall Stewart in his *Hawthorne: A Biography* (1948), pp. 169–70; and the reader may appropriately be invited to read *Melville's Religious Thought* . . . , by William Braswell (1943), one of the best books of a rare species.

3. I have not attempted to deal with Hawthorne's novels in this chapter because I have done so, by varying methods, in *Rage for Order* (1948), pp. 84–103—an essay which concerns itself chiefly with *The House of the Seven Gables*—and "*The Scarlet Letter:* A Literary Exercise in Moral Theology," *The Southern Review* (New Series), 1 (1965).

HENRY JAMES

The Jameses were of Albany, of Washington Square, New York, of Europe, of Boston and Cambridge, Mass.: migratory, partly because of the father's artificial leg, which required cities and pavements, partly by virtue of the father's having no business or profession, partly because of their being a world unto themselves.

These circumstances adequately account for James's tone in his novels and short stories laid in New England. It is always that of a cultivated outsider—something which he was long before he took up permanent residence in England. But James was an outsider in England, too: his triumph was one version of what his father was always concerned about: that of the conversion of waste. Henry had to learn to make his outsiderness an advantage in disinterested observation—something which emerges most clearly in the novels of the last period.

To the New England fictions should certainly be added James's 1879 monograph on Hawthorne, written for the "English Men of Letters" series, a brilliant critical study. Its best pages, perhaps, are those which deal with Hawthorne's relation to "the Puritan conscience": these pages will be found in the third chapter.

MARY E. WILKINS

There is a good monograph (chiefly biographical) on Miss Wilkins by Edward Foster (1956). This 'local color' writer was prolific. I have taken my illustrations from her early—and best—volumes, *A Humble Romance and Other Stories* (1887) and *A New England Nun and Other Stories* (1891).

HENRY ADAMS

One of the really good 'family' books is *The Adams Family* (1930), by James Truslow Adams, who makes it conscientiously clear that he is not of their clan. Henry and his brother Brooks (on whom there is an excellent monograph by Arthur F. Beringause [1955]) were grandsons of John Quincy Adams. They were, immensely, a writing family, the Adamses; and yet only in Henry does this propensity fully emerge.

Henry Adams is hard to 'classify'—a part, surely, of his interest. Elizabeth Stevenson's *A Henry Adams Reader* (1958) is probably the best introduction to this versatile, restless, learned, gifted, always searching late-Puritan, intent on discovering the meaning of existence.

His *Education of Henry Adams*, like his *Mont-Saint-Michel and Chartres*, was written for private circulation. The strange gap in *The Education* (one of twenty years) is never explained to the few intended readers, who understood the break in Adams' world caused by the suicidal death of his wife. She never appears, living or dead, in the autobiography, which is, anyway, an *intellectual* autobiography.

Helpful indeed—works of intelligence and taste—are the three volumes of biography by Ernest Samuels (1948, 1958, and 1964) and the 1957 monograph by J. C. Levenson, *The Mind and Art of Henry Adams*.

EDWIN ARLINGTON ROBINSON

Robinson is a poet hard to 'come by,' to decipher. The *Collected Poems* (1937) runs to nearly 1,500 pages of small print —too much for a poet who has to be closely read if at all. Some of this—chiefly, the long poems—is New England industry and New England mannerism: style dilating manner and motif. The long poems are too long; the anthologized short poems like "Richard Cory" too short (i.e., too much depending on a neat irony which does not invite rereading). And Robinson, a shy man, has many ways of hiding himself. It has also to be added that he hasn't had very good fortune in the critics he has attracted, who have more often been professors than poets and have taken him as a philosopher.

Averse as I generally am to the 'biographical approach,' I

think one needs to make some use of it with Robinson. I can offer thanks for the biography by Hermann Hagedorn, the poet's friend for twenty-five years (1938) and for Emory Neff's *Robinson* (1948); and there are two volumes, *Selected Letters . . .*, edited by Ridgely Torrence (1940) and *Untriangulated Stars . . .*, edited by Denham Sutcliffe (1947), both worth reading.

Largely unmarred by crochets and intelligently sympathetic is Yvor Winters' short critical book on Robinson (1946).

INDEX

INDEX

INDEX